PROBLEMS OF THE MODERN ECONOMY

The Battle Against Unemployment

PROBLEMS OF THE MODERN ECONOMY

General Editor: EDMUND S. PHELPS, *Yale University*

Each volume in this series presents
prominent positions in the debate of
an important issue of economic policy

THE BATTLE AGAINST UNEMPLOYMENT

CHANGING PATTERNS IN FOREIGN
  TRADE AND PAYMENTS

THE GOAL OF ECONOMIC GROWTH

MONOPOLY POWER AND ECONOMIC
  PERFORMANCE

PRIVATE WANTS AND PUBLIC NEEDS

THE UNITED STATES AND THE
  DEVELOPING ECONOMIES

LABOR AND THE NATIONAL ECONOMY

INEQUALITY AND POVERTY

The Battle
Against
Unemployment

Edited with an introduction by
ARTHUR M. OKUN
COUNCIL OF ECONOMIC ADVISERS
and YALE UNIVERSITY

NEW YORK
W · W · NORTON & COMPANY · INC ·

Library of Congress Catalog Card No. 63-21711

ALL RIGHTS RESERVED

Published simultaneously in the Dominion of
Canada by George J. McLeod Limited, Toronto

"Dimensions of the Employment Problem" by Albert Rees: from *A Symposium on Employment*, The American Banker's Association (Washington, D.C., 1964).

"The Great Unemployment Fallacy" by Edwin L. Dale, Jr.: from *The New Republic*, September 5, 1964. Copyright © 1964 Harrison-Blaine, Inc.

"National Economic Goals" and "Toward a Flexible Tax Policy" by the Commission on Money and Credit: from *Money & Credit: Their Influence on Jobs, Prices and Growth.* Copyright © 1961. Reprinted by permission of Prentice-Hall, Inc., Englewood Cliffs, N.J.

"The Case for High-pressure Economics" by Alvin H. Hansen: from Chs. 2 and 3 of *The American Economy.* Copyright © 1957 by McGraw-Hill Book Company. Reprinted by permission.

"The Case against High-pressure Economics" by Henry C. Wallich and "The Case for an Automatic Monetary Pilot" by Edward S. Shaw: pp. 116–136 and 59–68 from *United States Monetary Policy*, first edition, The American Assembly, Columbia University, 1958.

"The Threat of Inflationary Psychology" by Arthur F. Burns: "Monetary Policy and the Threat of Inflation," an address to the Fourteenth American Assembly, Arden House, Harriman, New York, October 18, 1958. Reprinted in *United States Monetary Policy*, 1st ed., The American Assembly, Columbia University.

"Our Menu of Policy Changes" by Paul A. Samuelson and Robert M. Solow: from "The Analytics of Anti-Inflationary Policy" from *Proceedings of the American Economic Association*, May 1960.

"The Problems of Our Price Indexes" by Richard Ruggles and "Computing the Consumer Price Index" by Ewan Clague: from *Challenge*, November 1961 and May 1962, The Magazine of Economic Affairs, a publication of the Institute of Economic Affairs, New York University.

"Weak Links in the Multiplier Chain" by Milton Friedman: from *Capitalism and Freedom.* Copyright © 1962 by The University of Chicago Press. Reprinted by permission.

"Functional Fiscal Policy for the 1960s" by Paul A. Samuelson: from *Stability and Growth in the American Economy*, copyright 1963 by the Wicksell Lecture Society, Stockholm, Sweden.

"The Need for Balanced Federal Budgets" by Maurice H. Stans: from *The Annals of the American Academy of Political and Social Science*, Vol. 326, November 1959. Reprinted by permission of the author and the Academy.

"The Limitations of Public Works" by Wilfred Lewis, Jr.: "Public Works and Postwar Recessions" from *Challenge*, November 1961, The Magazine of Economic Affairs, a publication of the Institute of Economic Affairs, New York University.

"The Formation of Fiscal Policy: 1953–1954" by Robert J. Donovan: from *Eisenhower: The Inside Story.* Coypright © 1956 by the New York Herald Tribune, Inc. Reprinted with the permission of Harper & Row, Publishers, Inc.

"The Tax-cut Harvest" by James Tobin: from *The New Republic*, March 7, 1964. Copyright © 1964 Harrison-Blaine, Inc.

"Monetary Policy and Economic Research" by Harry G. Johnson: "Monetary Theory and Policy" from *American Economic Review*, June 1962. Copyright 1962 by the American Economic Association.

"The Postwar Record of Monetary Policy" by Henry C. Wallich and Stephen H. Axilrod: pp. 91–99 from *United States Monetary Policy*, rev. ed. by Neil H. Jacoby, The American Assembly, Columbia University, 1958. Reprinted by permission of Frederick A. Praeger, Inc.

PRINTED IN THE UNITED STATES OF AMERICA

Contents

PART FOUR: Monetary Policy   160

Introduction

PROSPERITY IS RIVALED only by peace as the key political issue in the United States. Unemployment and recession hit people hard in their pockets and pocketbooks and threaten their freedom of action and security. Sustained economic expansion throughout the Kennedy-Johnson Administration was advanced by President Johnson as a strong argument for a Democratic vote in 1964. In contrast, after the 1960 election, former Vice President Richard M. Nixon expressed his feeling that the high unemployment of the 1960 recession had cost him the Presidency. Public action to curb unemployment lies in the sphere of political economy—both political values and economic analysis are essential ingredients in decision-making. Without assuming a set of social values, an economist cannot tell the nation what to do. Nevertheless economic analysis does have much light to throw on the issues. This volume opens with the late President Kennedy's eloquent warning that ideology and mythology obscure issues and his plea for an informed, dispassionate discussion of alternative routes to prosperity and high employment.

While the selections in this volume reach different conclusions on matters of fact and value, they all follow the spirit of social scientific inquiry that Kennedy commended. The essays in this volume also reflect the spirit of the Employment Act of 1946, which declared, "it is the continuing policy and responsibility of the Federal Government . . . to promote maximum employment, production, and purchasing power." The Employment Act committed the federal government to a policy of combating unemployment. The conclusion that social action to curb unemployment is necessary and desirable is neither trite nor self-evident. Thirty-five years ago most economists believed that the private enterprise system, functioning competitively, had an automatic tendency to balance supply and demand in the aggregate at the right level. Wide fluctuations in economic activity and excessive unemployment were generally interpreted as either inevitable features of a growing economy or the results of government interference in economic life. Such views pointed toward a hands-off policy of neutrality for the government.

The Great Depression had a permanent impact on attitudes toward public policy against unemployment. At the depths of the depression, one-fourth of the nation's labor force was unemployed; and the unemployment rate did not fall below 14 percent throughout the 1930s. No individual escaped the impact of this great collapse and no individual could combat it on his own. With the sole exception of the Civil War, no episode in our nation's history has so strained the very fabric of American society. The public refused to accept this deep and persistent depression as inevitable; nor could it be convinced that the depression was attributable to the errors of the government. The call for social action was insistent and persuasive; it was answered by the innovations of the New Deal. Meanwhile, at a theoretical level, the great British economist John Maynard Keynes dealt a mortal blow to Say's Law, the doctrine that supply creates its own demand; he thereby destroyed the logical foundation for faith in the basic stability of the private economy. Thus, the battle of public policy against unemployment took shape in the 1930s.

The battle was resumed under the banner of the Employment Act after 1946. The postwar employment record is far superior to that of earlier years. Indeed, in the first postwar decade, unemployment rates of 4 percent and lower were the rule, broken only during and immediately after two brief recessions. From late 1957 to 1964, however, unemployment was not significantly below 5 percent at any time; it averaged nearly 6 percent.

UNEMPLOYMENT: CAUSES AND CONSEQUENCES

This backsliding in our performance has been the subject of much discussion and investigation, reflected in the articles in Part One. The report of Senator Eugene R. McCarthy's Special Committee on Unemployment Problems translates unemployment statistics into concrete human terms, revealing the economic and psychological hardships of joblessness. In his own essay the editor of this volume discusses and estimates the cost of excessive unemployment in terms of the loss of potential production, underlining the economic waste associated with the increased unemployment rate. An important issue in Part One is the level of a feasible employment target under present conditions. The editor takes the 4-percent unemployment rate as a benchmark for full employment. Albert Rees also finds the 4-percent rate appealing, although he points out that its appeal comes from history rather than logic: "We have reached it before during peacetime and without an unacceptable rate of price inflation." Rees discusses the frictional and structural factors that prevent us from setting more ambitious goals even though most other highly developed nations achieve lower unemployment rates. He also investigates our failure to reach the 4-percent target in recent years and concludes, "Structural factors will go only a small part of the way in explaining our present situation. We are left with lack of demand as the remaining and major cause of high unemployment."

Charles C. Killingsworth takes a different position: "Before we could get down to an over-all unemployment rate as low as 4 percent, we would have a severe shortage of workers at the top of the educational ladder." According to his analysis, automation has twisted the pattern of demand for labor, creating a potential shortage of the highly skilled and highly educated but an excess supply of the unskilled. With such a structural imbalance, expansionary fiscal and monetary policies may create inflationary excess demands in some labor markets without significantly remedying the slack in other markets. Killingsworth's analysis points toward a less ambitious unemployment target until we can implement the necessary manpower and educational policies to expand the supply of skilled labor. Edwin L. Dale, Jr., argues strongly against this "structuralist" interpretation of the higher unemployment rates of recent years. He contends that with a new determination to use expansionary fiscal policy, the United States can and will bring its unemployment rate down below 4 percent in the next few years.

In the debate on the causes of higher unemployment, it should be recognized that structural policies and over-all demand policies are not necessarily competing alternatives. Whether or not structural unemployment has actually increased in recent years, we should be eager to improve education, training, and mobility so as to reduce structural unemployment in future years.

THE GOALS: EMPLOYMENT AND PRICE STABILITY

In setting an employment target, we must evaluate the effects of higher or lower unemployment on other objectives. High employment is not the only economic goal of our society. Price stability is another economic objective, and one that may conflict with high employment. If a measure to increase employment would at the same time raise prices, we must balance the gains and losses. The selections of Part Two are concerned with this issue.

The report of the Commission on Money and Credit assesses the goals of high employment, price stability, and economic growth; it concludes that they are all compatible if we choose the right mix of policy and "if we do not expect the impossible for each." The last qualification really concedes that conflicts may arise and difficult decisions on the trade-offs may be required. If one goal is given a definite priority over the others, a conflict does appear. To get maximum insurance against inflation, we would have to depress demand and tolerate high unemployment rates. On the other hand, to attain very low levels of unemployment rapidly, we would have to accept rapid inflation. Optimal policy is a balance of risks: the right level of demand is a narrow line between the specter of inflation from too much demand and the danger of excessive unemployment from too little demand. Any time we are free of one of these concerns, it must mean that we are unduly sacrificing the other objective.

In his essay, Alvin H. Hansen urges us to create a high-pressure economy, accepting the risks of inflation rather than the dangers of stagnation. He argues that the evils of inflation have often been exaggerated and that an attempt to ensure absolute price stability would gravely weaken our long-term economic performance. While recognizing that no formula for balancing the risks can rest on a firm analytical foundation, Hansen offers his own preferred rule: tolerate price increases "so long as percentage increases of aggregate output exceed the percentage increases in the price level." That rule does not satisfy Henry C. Wallich. He points to the risks of hyperinflation, economic collapse, and price controls that may stem from tolerance of "creeping inflation." He recognizes the appeal of more output and more employment in the short run but warns that the "chickens may come home to roost." On Wallich's side of the high-pressure low-pressure debate is Arthur F. Burns, who stresses "the growing belief in the inevitability of inflation" and its danger, and calls for an amendment of the Employment Act to include "reasonable stability of the consumer price level" explicitly among the objectives of policy. Burns' essay also contains what has proven to be a timely mention of the importance of price stability to our international position.

Both Burns and Wallich wrote these essays in 1958. Since then, a balance-of-payments problem has confronted the United States, giving us added reason to battle against inflation. But during the same period, our performance on prices has much improved. Wholesale prices in 1964 are no higher than they were in 1958, and the consumer price index has moved up very moderately, a bit more than 1 percent a year. In retrospect, most economists would conclude that unemployment—not inflation—has been our major economic problem since 1957. With 20-20 hindsight, most of us would conclude that our policies tolerated excessive unemployment and should have taken more expansionary risks from 1957 to 1963.

Paul A. Samuelson and Robert M. Solow appraise our choices for the future. Using the analytical device of a Phillips curve, they present us with a menu of policy choices that will not permit us to have our cake and eat it too. To ensure absolute price stability, they estimate that a 5½-percent unemployment rate must be tolerated. To achieve a 3-percent unemployment rate, we would have to accept inflation of 4–5 percent a year. According to their analysis, the simultaneous pursuit of both full employment and price stability creates a very real dilemma.

Richard Ruggles, however, suggests that this dilemma may be partly a figment of our price indices rather than a fact of life. He contends that because quality changes and new products are not adequately measured, our price statistics move upward even when there is no true erosion of the buying power of the consumer's dollar. But the Commissioner of Labor Statistics, Ewan Clague, disagrees; he sees no reason why the flaws of our price indices should produce a consistent upward bias.

FISCAL POLICY

Fiscal and monetary policies are the principal weapons in the battle against unemployment. Part Three is devoted to fiscal policy. Because private demand has a reliable tendency to fluctuate, our fiscal policies should be flexible. At times private demand will show great strength and spur the economy forward; at other times it will slacken. Rigid fiscal-monetary policies will let fluctuations in private demand destabilize over-all economic activity, creating either intolerable inflation or excessive unemployment. To contribute to economic stability and to help maintain the ideal target of utilization, public policies should compensate for the fluctuations in private demand. When businessmen are trying to invest more than the public would be willing to save at high employment, the government can contribute to stability through fiscal policy by enlarging its saving or budget surplus. When on the other hand private saving tends to outrun investment at full utilization, the government contributes to over-all balance in the economy by increasing its dissaving or budget deficits. The objective of balance in the economy as a whole will argue sometimes for government surpluses and sometimes for government deficits but rarely for a precise balance in the federal budget. Moreover, because both the size and the composition of the budget also influence economic activity, a balanced budget is no criterion for fiscal neutrality. These are the tenets of "functional finance" set forth by Professor Samuelson in his article on fiscal policy.

The mechanics of expansionary fiscal policy are explained in the Council of Economic Advisers' discussion of the multiplier. Budgetary policies can raise the take-home pay of the American public—through tax reduction, increased transfer payments, or increased government purchases of goods and services. Since households gear their outlays to their disposable incomes, they will increase their expenditures for consumer goods and for services, thus generating more income for others and further increases in demand. Furthermore, the gains in sales, profits, and retained business earnings will encourage investment. Whether expansionary fiscal policy is good or bad depends on the state of the economy. When there are idle resources, increases in total spending are likely to be translated into more employment and production. When resources are fully employed, however, added demand will primarily raise prices, not employment and real GNP. This Keynesian analysis of the multiplier process is at the heart of the belief that budgetary policies have important effects on the economy.

Milton Friedman contests this central tenet of functional finance, questioning the potency of fiscal measures. According to Friedman, many links in the multiplier chain are weak and they render fiscal policy an unreliable and ineffective technique of stabilization.

In contrast, former Budget Director Maurice H. Stans does not doubt the power of the federal budget but rather emphasizes the likelihoood that it may be used to produce harmful results. Stans believes that once the rule of budget-balancing is ignored, deficits become much more likely than surpluses for political reasons; ignoring the rule thus creates a bias toward inflation. He is also concerned that departure from the balanced-budget rule leaves no guide to decisions on public expenditure and may lead to an irreversible growth of the public sector. It is interesting to note that Stans's case for balanced budgets does not stress the burden of the public debt. Certain effects—indeed, possible burdens—of the public debt are recognized in professional thinking, but economists agree that an internal public debt is not analogous to a national mortgage. If the average American baby is born with a $1600 burden of national debt on his back, he is also born with a $1600 silver spoon of public-debt holdings in his mouth.

Despite dissenting opinions, fiscal policy has won acceptance as a tool for promoting economic stability. There remain, nevertheless, highly important issues on the proper choice, size, and timing of fiscal instruments. Through the New Deal and the early postwar recessions, public works received top billing among the various means of generating employment and getting the multiplier process into action. Wilfred Lewis, Jr., nevertheless concludes that countercyclical public-works measures have played only a limited role in promoting economic stability in the postwar period. Moreover, he argues, the time lags associated with them, and the difficulty of reversing action, significantly, curtail their usefulness in a mild and short-lived recession. These difficulties are reflected in Robert J. Donovan's chronicle of cabinet meetings in the 1954 recession. For the first time, a Republican President fought a recession with many of the measures that had previously been associated with the New Deal and Keynesian economics. President Eisenhower was prepared to increase public works and the deficit and "to err on the side of doing too much rather than too little." But it was not easy to make fine expansionary adjustments of federal expenditures. Highway construction seemed to be the most promising line of attack, but it was clearly slow acting and irreversible.

The limitations of public works as a counterrecession measure are one reason for a shift of emphasis to tax policy. The higher tax rates of the postwar period are another reason. Since federal taxes were only 3½ percent of the Gross National Product in 1929, the opportunities for a stimulus from a tax cut were limited. Today there is much more room for tax reduction. High rates of taxation have also contributed as an automatic stabilizer to the performance of our economy. As the second selection from the Commission on Money and Credit report points out, federal tax receipts share significantly in any economic decline or expansion. A dollar drop in the GNP means substantially lower government receipts, and hence much less than a dollar reduction in private disposable income. As a result, the multiplier is reduced in size and the economy is more stable. Unemployment compensation is another important shock absorber for disposable income during recessions.

These built-in stabilizers limit the magnitude of a decline, but they cannot, in general, reverse the direction of economic trends. For such a task, discretionary changes in tax rates are required. With the exception of the 1954, when the temporary Korean-war tax increases were allowed to expire, tax reduction has never been used as an antirecessionary device. To encourage the use of tax reduction in attacking recession, the Commission on Money and Credit proposed congressional action to vest the President with conditional powers to reduce taxes, subject to congressional veto. The proposal was designed to guarantee swift action that would make tax policy a more attractive, more appealing, and more effective device for promoting economic stability. The proposal also appealed to some conservatives who favored tax cuts during a recession as an alternative to increased government expenditures. But to date the commission's proposal has had little appeal to the Congress. It represents a marked shift in the division of powers between the executive and legislative branches of our government. A variant of the proposal was explicitly recommended by President Kennedy in 1962, but it was not enacted.

The shifting emphasis in the use of fiscal tools was most vividly evident in the Kennedy Administration's proposal for a substantial tax cut during a period of economic expansion in 1963. The intent of the proposal was to invigorate the expansion and reduce unemployment. The tax cut was enacted early in 1964 as President Lyndon Johnson's first major legislative victory. The next two selections appraise the tax cut. James Tobin hails it as a "victory for a rational fiscal policy." While Professor Burns expresses some concern that this large dose of fiscal medicine may overstimulate the economy, he is enthusiastic about the principle of tax reduction and sets forth a proposal for repeated smaller doses.

MONETARY POLICY

The other major set of instruments to promote economic stability is that of monetary policy. The Board of Governors of the Federal Reserve System has powers to influence the cost and availability of credit and the liquidity of the economy through its open-market operations, its discount-rate policy, and its power to vary reserve requirements for member banks. The actions of the central bank can have widespread repercussions on financial markets and thereby affect all types of investment decisions. The mechanisms by which the actions of the central bank influence the economy are explained in the selection prepared by the Board of Governors. The board claims to have no magic for monetary policy, but it does portray its actions as a beneficial contribution to economic stability.

With the renewed use of monetary policy in the post-Korean period has come increased attention to money in the professional literature. Economists still have much to learn about monetary policy—how fast it works, how much effect it has on the economy, and where it exercises its major impact. Major efforts by economic researchers to investigate these key issues are discussed in the article by Harry G. Johnson.

In reviewing the postwar record of U.S. monetary policy,

Professor Wallich and Stephen H. Axilrod point out how concern about debt management blocked the Federal Reserve from
exercising appropriate anti-inflationary measures in the early postwar years. They then consider the record from 1951–1958 and
conclude that the Federal Reserve deserves a high but not perfect score for its actions during this period. The monetary
authorities faced a major dilemma in 1957 when unemployment
began to increase while prices were still rising. More recently,
conflicting international and domestic objectives have confronted
the Fed. While low short-term interest rates encourage U.S.
dollars to go abroad in search of a higher yield, high interest
rates and tight money endanger economic expansion at home.
Wallich and Axilrod judge the monetary authorities favorably
on their performance in a difficult situation.

Edward S. Shaw is much less satisfied about the past record
and the future potentialities of discretionary monetary policy. He
sets forth a proposal for replacing monetary management with
an automatic system to provide for a regular and smooth percentage expansion of the money supply. In Shaw's view, this new
automatic stabilizer would be more valuable than the judgment
of Federal Reserve authorities. While he believes that changes in
the money supply are powerful influences on the economy, he
doubts that discretionary changes can lead to the right amount
of money at the right time. Shaw's automatic rule is criticized by
Professor Samuelson; he contends that the rule rests on a dubious quantity-theory framework and that Shaw's skeptical appraisal of the judgment of monetary managers is not justified.

Beginning in 1961, the American economy experienced a
long, sustained expansion of business activity, which dramatically
reversed the trend toward frequent recessions in the 1950s. From
the low point of the 1960–61 recession to the end of 1964, output
grew by one fifth, or more than $100 billion (measured in 1964
prices).

The advances in economic performance have been matched
by advances in economic policy. Measures to stabilize the economy
have played an important role in supporting the economic upswing. Early in the Kennedy Administration, substantial increases
in federal spending, required principally for defense and space,
had an expansionary influence; then tax reduction became the principal expansionary instrument. Depreciation rules for taxation

were liberalized in 1962; then a 7-percent tax credit on business investment in machinery and equipment was enacted; and finally, the Revenue Act of 1964 reduced personal income taxes by one fifth, on the average, and corporate income taxes by nearly one tenth. Meanwhile, the Federal Reserve has avoided the increases in long-term interest rates and the tightening of credit that have typically accompanied the rising financial demands of an economic expansion.

As a result, there is increasing agreement that the government can contribute positively and decisively to the strength of prosperity in a free economy. There is less fatalism about the rhythm of the business cycle and more determination to head off threats of recession or of an unsuitable boom.

But our problems are far from solved. While unemployment has improved to the extent that gains in production have exceeded the rise in our productive capacity, 5 percent of the labor force still remains jobless. And our record of price stability has yet to be tested in an environment of full utilization. Much work remains ahead of us to achieve complete victory in the battle against unemployment.

PROBLEMS OF THE MODERN ECONOMY

The Battle Against Unemployment

PROLOGUE

Mythology vs. Economic Knowledge

JOHN F. KENNEDY

This selection is from the late President Kennedy's commencement address at Yale University on June 11, 1962. In it, he called for informed, dispassionate discussion of key economic problems and pointed to the issues discussed in this volume.

THE GREAT ENEMY of the truth is very often not the lie—deliberate, contrived and dishonest—but the myth—persistent, persuasive and unrealistic. Too often we hold fast to the clichés of our forebears. We subject all facts to a prefabricated set of interpretations. We enjoy the comfort of opinion without the discomfort of thought.

Mythology distracts us everywhere—in government as in business, in politics as in economics, in foreign affairs as in domestic policy. But I want to particularly consider the myth and reality in our national economy. In recent months many have come to feel, as I do, that the dialogue between the parties—between business and government—is clogged by illusion and platitude and fails to reflect the true realities of contemporary American society. . . .

Let us turn to the problem of our fiscal policy. Here the myths are legion and the truth hard to find. But let me take as a prime example the problem of the federal budget. We persist in measuring our federal fiscal integrity today by the conventional or administrative budget—with results which would be regarded as absurd in any business firm—in any country of Europe—or in any careful assessment of the reality of our national finances. The administrative budget has sound administrative uses. But for wider purposes it is less helpful. It omits our special trust funds; it neglects changes in assets or inventories; it cannot tell a loan from a straight expenditure; and, worst of all, it cannot distinguish between operating expenditures and long-term investments.

This budget—in relation to the great problems of federal fiscal policy—is not simply irrelevant; it can be actively misleading. And yet there is a mythology that measures all of our national soundness or unsoundness on the single simple basis of this same annual administrative budget. If our federal budget is to serve, not the debate, but the country, we must and will find ways of clarifying this area of discourse.

Still in the area of fiscal policy, let me say a word about deficits. The myth persists that federal deficits create inflation and budget surpluses prevent it. Yet sizable budget surpluses after the war did not prevent inflation, and persistent deficits for the last several years have not upset our basic price stability. Obviously deficits are sometimes dangerous—and so are surpluses. But honest assessment plainly requires a more sophisticated view than the old and automatic cliché that deficits automatically bring inflation.

There are myths also about our public debt. It is widely supposed that this debt is growing at a dangerously rapid rate. In fact, both the debt per person and the debt as a proportion of our gross national product have declined sharply since the Second World War. In absolute terms the national debt increased only 8 percent, while private debt was increasing 305 percent, and the debts of state and local governments increased 378 percent. Moreover, debts, public and private, are neither good nor bad, in and of themselves. Borrowing can lead to overextension and collapse—but it can also lead to expansion and strength. There is no single, simple slogan in this field that we can trust.

Finally, I come to the problem of confidence. Confidence is a matter of myth and also a matter of truth—and this time let me take the truth of the matter first.

It is true—and of high importance—that the prosperity of this country depends on assurance that all major elements within it will live up to their responsibilities. If business were to neglect its obligations to the public; if labor were blind to all public responsibility; above all, if government were to abandon its obvious

—and statutory—duty of watchful concern for our economic health—if any of these things should happen, then confidence might well be weakened and the danger of stagnation would increase. This is the true issue of confidence.

But there is also the false issue—and its simplest form is the assertion that any and all unfavorable turns of the speculative wheel—however temporary and however plainly speculative in character—are the result of "lack of confidence in the national administration." This I must tell you, while comforting, is not wholly true. Worse, it obscures the reality—which is also simple. The solid ground of mutual confidence is the necessary partnership of government with all of the sectors of our society in the steady quest for economic progress.

Corporate plans are not based on a political confidence in party leaders but on an economic confidence in the nation's ability to invest and produce and consume. Business had full confidence in the Administrations in power in 1929, 1954, 1958, and 1960—but this was not enough to prevent recession when business lacked full confidence in the economy. What matters is the capacity of the nation as a whole to deal with its economic problems and its opportunities.

The stereotypes I have been discussing distract our attention and divide our effort. These stereotypes do our nation a disservice, not just because they are exhausted and irrelevant, but above all because they are misleading—because they stand in the way of the solution of hard and complicated problems. It is not new that past debates should obscure present realities. But the damage of such a false dialogue is greater today than ever before simply because today the safety of all the world—the very future of freedom—depends as never before upon the sensible and clear-headed management of the domestic affairs of the United States.

The real issues of our time are rarely so dramatic as the issues of the age of Calhoun. The differences today are usually matters of degree. And we cannot understand and attack our contemporary problems in 1962 if we are bound by traditional labels and worn-out slogans of an earlier era. The unfortunate fact of the matter is that our rhetoric has not kept pace with the speed of social and economic change. Our political debates, our public discourse—on current domestic and economic issues—too often bear little or no relation to the actual problems the United States faces.

What is at stake in our economic decisions today is, not some grand warfare of rival ideologies which will sweep the country with passion, but the practical management of a modern economy. What we need is not labels and clichés but more basic discussion of the sophisticated and technical questions involved in keeping a great economic machine moving ahead.

The national interest lies in high employment and steady expansion of output, in stable prices, and a strong dollar. The declaration of such objectives is easy; their attainment in an intricate and interdependent economy and world is a little more difficult. To attain them, we require not automatic response but hard thought. Let me end by suggesting a few of the real questions on our national agenda.

How can our budget and tax policies supply adequate revenues and preserve our balance of payments position without slowing up our economic growth?

How are we to set our interest rates and regulate the flow of money in ways which will stimulate the economy at home, without weakening the dollar abroad? Given the spectrum of our domestic and international responsibilities, what should be the mix between fiscal and monetary policy?

With the necessity of maintaining our competitive position in the world, what should be the price and wage policies of our basic industries? Is there a public interest in such price and wage decisions, and, if so, how is it to be defined and organized and expressed?

How can we develop and sustain strong and stable world markets for basic commodities without unfairness to the consumer and without undue stimulus to the producer?

How can we generate the buying power which can consume what we produce on our farms and in our factories?

How can we take advantage of the miracles of automation with the great demand that it will put upon highly skilled labor and yet offer employment to the half million of unskilled school dropouts each year which enter the labor market, eight million of them in the 1960s?

How do we eradicate the barriers which separate substantial

minorities of our citizens from access to education and employment on equal terms with the rest?

How, in sum, can we make our free economy work at full capacity—that is, provide adequate profits for enterprise, adequate wages for labor, adequate utilization of plant and adequate opportunity for all?

These are the problems that we should be talking about—that the political parties and the various groups in our country should be discussing. They cannot be solved by incantations from the forgotten past. But the example of Western Europe shows that they are capable of solution—that governments, and many of them are conservative governments, prepared to face technical problems without ideological preconceptions, can coordinate the elements of a national economy to bring about growth and prosperity—a decade of it.

Some conversations I have heard in our own country sound like old records, long-playing, left over from the middle Thirties. The debate of the Thirties had its great significance and produced great results. But it took place in a different world with different needs and different tasks. It is our responsibility today to live in our own world—and to identify the needs and discharge the tasks of the 1960s.

If there is any current trend toward meeting present problems with old clichés, this is the moment to stop it—before it lands us all in a bog of sterile acrimony. . . .

PART ONE

Unemployment: Concepts,
Causes, and Consequences

The Costs of Unemployment

SENATE SPECIAL COMMITTEE
ON UNEMPLOYMENT PROBLEMS

This selection is from the 1960 report of the Senate Special Committee on Unemployment Problems; Senator Eugene J. Mc-Carthy of Minnesota served as chairman.

WHETHER MEASURED by economic and material loss or by human suffering and wasted skills, the cost of unemployment is high. Unused natural resources remain to be used in the future. But work, the creative activity of man, once wasted can never be recovered; what might have been produced is lost. The damage to individuals and to society from unemployment often cannot be repaired.

THE ECONOMIC COST TO THE INDIVIDUAL AND HIS FAMILY

Nine out of ten workers in the United States are members of families with responsibility for the support of other members. Nearly half of the 44 million families in the United States in 1957 were supported by the efforts of one wage earner; 45 percent had two or more wage earners; 5 percent had income exclusively from pensions, investments, or social welfare assistance.

The financial problems of the families of the unemployed have never been fully or accurately studied, but a number of State unemployment bureaus have made intensive studies of spending patterns before and during unemployment. A sampling of unemployment compensation beneficiaries in Oregon in 1958 showed that 37 percent of the beneficiaries interviewed were heads of families for whom unemployment benefits were the only reported regular family income. Another 17 percent lived alone and were totally dependent upon unemployment compensation. Twenty-one percent were normally the chief wage earners in families which had, however, other wage earners.

Many families in the United States are dependent upon the earnings of two or more members or have adjusted their standards of living to the earnings of two or more members. Loss of job by any member contributing to the income of the family forces economic and social adjustment for everyone; in some cases it may even endanger family welfare.

Loss of jobs by the many individuals who do not qualify for unemployment insurance benefits usually means a complete loss of income, but even those who are eligible for benefits suffer a drastic reduction in income. In 1959, for example, unemployment insurance benefits averaged about $30 a week; very few of the unemployed who received unemployment benefits received more than half of their previous income.

Unemployment benefits for many are quickly exhausted. During the 1958 business downturn about two-thirds of the unemployed received benefits, but in the last part of 1959 fewer than half the unemployed collected benefits. Family incomes during these periods must, of course, be supplemented from other sources. Other members of the family may be able to get jobs, small family-farm production may be increased, or tenants may be taken into the family home.

Social security payments are particularly important as a source of income for older workers who become unemployed. Persons between 65 and 72 years old cannot collect these pensions if they continue to work, except at relatively low pay, but if they lose their jobs they become eligible at once. Old age and survivors insurance is important as a source of family income only if the recipient is a member of a family. Since many pension recipients live with their children or other relatives, some pensions do help support unemployed relatives.

Family investments and savings, including insurance policies, are another source of income during times of stress. According to a Michigan study introduced into the record during the committee hearings in Detroit,

About 44 percent of the unemployed heads of families reported that they had some savings which they used in the emergency. Although the extent of the savings drawn is not known, reliance upon savings was by far the most important measure taken. . . . This fact indicates the extent to which thrift and self-responsibility are relied upon to meet unemployment emergencies.

Measures taken to adjust to loss of income, according to the same study, were, in the order of importance: use of savings, reductions in buying, getting help from relatives, piling up bills, and borrowing money. Some families moved to cheaper quarters, were able to have another member of the family go to work, or sought relief from a public welfare agency. The average family took two of these measures. The major areas for economizing were clothing, recreational and community activities, food, insurance, living quarters, and postponement of medical or dental care.

The effects of unemployment are felt long after the unemployed person has gone back to work. Accumulated debts have to be repaid, neglected health problems attended to, and depleted savings replenished. In most cases it takes a family a long time to regain the financial position it held before unemployment.

THE SOCIAL EFFECTS OF UNEMPLOYMENT

Many serious social problems follow directly from unemployment. In some areas of chronic unemployment these problems are as bad now as they were during the depression of the 1930's. The social effects of unemployment vary considerably according to the age, length of unemployment, the economic level of the unemployed, and other factors, but there is a common pattern of unfortunate consequences.

Unemployment is, of course, the greatest hazard for people in the lowest social and income groups, whose members often hold short-term jobs and are subject to layoffs. The family's normal standard of living is low, and family life is often disorganized and unstable. Children generally leave school at an early age and the delinquency rate is high. One witness before the committee observed:

Except in those cases where there is obvious personal disability in either or both parents, the social scientist is reluctant to accept this as a normal situation. The cultural environment that is often the result of the unemployment situation also becomes a cause of unemployment as the employer sifts through the applications for the "right kind" of employee. This is obviously a vicious circle. This acts as a barricade to the normal aspirations of American people to move up into the broad middle class. The basic sociological question is whether we must necessarily and always have a residual category of people at the bottom of the social structure.

Unemployment also has serious effects upon citizens who consider themselves members of the middle class. For them unemployment carries a suggestion of failure, even though it may be the result of forces beyond the control of anyone in the family. Persons responsible for support of the family suffer loss of prestige and status. Members of the family are inclined to withdraw from participation in community and neighborhood activities, unions, lodges, and similar groups. One witness in Evansville, Ind., described the reaction in his own words:

I know all morning you have heard quite a bit about the financial status of the unemployed, but I would like to say a few words about the emotional status. . . . There is a social aspect to unemployment that arises from the ties and bonds of group relations and friends and neighbors and so on. Everybody wants to be recognized socially, and while I was unemployed, emotional problems did arise; for instance, with my friends, they knew I was unemployed and knew I could not afford to entertain, they didn't think I could afford it, and rather than ask us to go places with them, they wanted to save us the embarrassment and that leaves quite a problem of being under the pressure that we were under. I say "we"—my whole family was involved. It made us wonder if we were actually forsaken by our friends or if this was true friendship to ignore us.

The effect on the children of the unemployed is most distressing. Their health, security, educational opportunities, and entire future are endangered. In one county in West Virginia the school superintendent reported that one out of three pupils in a school enrollment of 22,374 came from a family in which the person who normally supported the family was unemployed; in the month of October 1959, 24.8 percent of the school lunches were free or sold at a reduced price. . . .

In another survey of 11 schools, the family head of 39 percent of the children was unemployed. Children in one school were weighed in November and again at the start of their Christmas vacation to measure the effect of the school's hot lunch program. The net gain of between 3 and 5 pounds per pupil was completely wiped out during the Christmas vacation when the children had to eat at home. . . .

An unemployed mine worker summarized his life and future this way:

The biggest majority of us never had an opportunity to get an education, so then we had to go into the mines at an early age—15, 16 years old. The biggest part of us are married and if we should leave here now and go to the city, what confronts us? If you're over 35 you can't get a job. And if a man's got a family and he goes to the city, what job can he get if he doesn't have any skill?

The director of the welfare department of St. Louis County in Minnesota reported:

In all too many families the stress of unemployment tends to separate rather than to mold the family into a smoother functioning unit. . . . The most important reaction is that there seems to be an increase in the hostile reaction toward one another and also toward society . . . the wife blames the husband for being out of work. . . . In many instances the roles become reversed. In many of these situations, the family is never able fully to recover, to the detriment of themselves and the community.

During fiscal year 1959, the Federal Government donated 700 million pounds of surplus foods to needy persons; in September 1959, more than 4 million persons in family units received donated commodities.

The problems of the underemployed are similar to those of the unemployed. In 1958, one-fourth of the 44 million families in the United States had annual cash incomes of less than $3,000; nearly one-fifth had incomes of less than $2,500.

Unemployment affects communities as well as families. If plants are closed, wages in other industries may be cut, retail sales drop, and plans to improve businesses and community facilities are often canceled. Property values generally decline and tax rates rise.

Many communities have made great efforts to solve their own problems. The adversity of unemployment often creates a common understanding and a community willingness to work together. This determination to rehabilitate a community was manifested strongly in the cooperative efforts of business, labor, and civic leaders in communities such as Evansville, Ind., and Scranton, Pa. In spite of the best efforts, however, the obstacles in most cases are too great for the community to overcome alone. One community leader in Pennsylvania expressed both the spirit of his community and the nature of the problem in these words:

It is an amazing thing that the unemployment, bad as it is, has not sapped or destroyed the spirit of the people in a community like this. . . . They are fighting and fighting very hard. . . . There is a great resource here in spirit and pride. There are institutions already built up, and I don't think we can today just casually walk away from them and abandon them and say we can put a steel mill or a factory in a field some place and the community will build up around it. . . . What sort of community will that be? . . . Which is easier to do, to build a community or to build an industry? . . . And which are the things that have the roots, the industrial plants or the people? . . . And these communities had their days when they were raw young communities without traditions . . . and now they are mature and can make a tremendous contribution to stability and to decency and to the morality of citizens, and do things for family life that a settled community can do, it is a shame if we just abandon them. . . . You probably will have to change a great deal of thinking, but I think we should not rule out some subsidies on a Government level to industries which will come into a place like this.

The economic and social costs of unemployment deserve far greater attention than they have received. Present measures to deal with unemployment and its consequences at the local, State, and Federal governmental levels are seriously inadequate.

The Gap between Actual and Potential Output

ARTHUR M. OKUN

This article is adapted from a paper which appeared in the 1962 Proceedings of the Business and Economic Statistics Section of the American Statistical Association. The technical statistical analysis in the original article is omitted here.

"How MUCH output can the economy produce under conditions of full employment?" The concept and measurement of potential GNP are addressed to this question. It is a question with policy significance because the pursuit of full employment (or "maximum employment" in the language of the Employment Act) is a goal of policy. And a target of full employment of labor needs to be linked to a corresponding target of full-employment output, since policy measures designed to influence employment operate by affecting aggregate demand and production. How far we stand from the target of full-employment output is important information in formulating fiscal and monetary policy. Thus, quantification of potential output offers one of the guides to stabilization policy and one indicator of its success.

The quantification of potential output—and the accompanying measure of the "gap" between actual and potential—is at best an uncertain estimate and not a firm, precise measure. While there are more precise measures of economic performance, they are not fully substitutable for the concept of potential output. To appraise the vigor of an expanding economy, it is important and enlightening to study customary cyclical measures, such as advance over previous peak levels or recession trough levels. But these measures do not tell us how far we have to go to meet our targets, unless we are prepared to assume that each peak is like any other one and all troughs are likewise uniform. The record of the past decade testifies to the dramatic differences among cyclical peaks in levels of resource utilization.

The evaluation of potential output can also help to point up the enormous social cost of idle resources. If programs to lower unemployment from 5½ to 4 percent of the labor force are viewed as attempts to raise the economy's "grade" from 94½ to 96, the case for them may not seem compelling. Focus on the "gap" helps to remind policy-makers of the large reward associated with such an improvement.

THE 4-PERCENT UNEMPLOYMENT RATE

Potential GNP is a supply concept, a measure of productive capacity. But it is not a measure of how much output could be generated by unlimited amounts of aggregate demand. The nation would probably be most productive in the short-run with inflationary pressure pushing the economy. But the social target of maximum production and employment is constrained by a social desire for price stability and free markets. The full-employment goal must be understood as striving for maximum production without inflationary pressure; or, more precisely, as aiming for a point of balance between more output and greater price stability, with appropriate regard for the social valuation of these two objectives.

It is interesting and perhaps surprising that there seems to be more agreement that a 4-percent unemployment rate is a reasonable target under existing labor-market conditions than on any of the analytical steps needed to justify such a conclusion. Economists have never developed a clear criterion of tolerable price behavior or a quantitative balancing of conflicting objectives which could be invoked to either support or attack the target of a 4-percent rate. Indeed, I should expect that many economists who agree on the 4-percent target would disagree in estimating how prices and wages would behave if we were on target. Nor can the 4-percent rate be said to meet Beveridge's criterion for full employment—that job vacancies should be equal to the number of unemployed. We simply have no count of job vacancies and could not possibly translate Beveridge's goal into any available measure of unemployment.

Having said what the 4-percent unemployment rate is not, I shall now state that it is the target rate of labor utilization underlying the calculation of potential GNP in this paper. The statistical and methodological problems would not be altered if a different rate were selected; only the numbers would be changed.

In estimating potential GNP, most of the facts about the economy are taken as they exist: technological knowledge, the capital stock, natural resources, the skill and education of the labor force are all data, rather than variables. Potential differs from actual only because the potential concept depends on the assumption—normally contrary to fact—that aggregate demand is exactly at the level that yields a rate of unemployment equal to 4 percent of the civilian labor force. If, in fact, aggregate demand is lower, part of potential GNP is not produced; there is unrealized potential or a "gap" between actual and potential output.

The failure to use one year's potential fully can influence future potential GNP: to the extent that low utilization rates and accompanying low profits and personal incomes hold down investment in plant, equipment, research, housing, and education, the growth of potential GNP will be retarded. Because today's actual output influences tomorrow's productive capacity, success in the stabilization objective promotes more rapid economic growth.

THE MEASUREMENT PROBLEM

As it has been defined above, potential output is observed only when the unemployment rate is 4 percent, and even then must be viewed as subject to random variation. At any other time, it must be regarded as a hypothetical magnitude. The observed actual measures of labor utilization tell us by a simple arithmetic calculation how much employment would have to increase, given the labor force, to make the unemployment rate 4 percent. But they do not offer similar direct information on other matters that might make labor input at full employment different from its observed level: (1) how average hours worked per man would be altered if the level of aggregate demand were consistent with full employment; (2) how participation rates in the labor force—and hence the size of the labor force—would be affected under conditions of full employment.

Nor do the data directly reveal what aggregate labor productivity would be under full-employment conditions. There are many reasons why productivity might be altered in the aggregate; the added workers, changed average hours, possible alterations in the sectoral distribution of employment, higher utilization rate of capital, and altered efficiency in the use of employees all could make a difference in productivity at full employment.

Ideally, the measurement of potential output would appraise the various possible influences of high employment on labor input and productivity and evaluate the influences step by step, developing quantitative estimates for each adjustment to produce the desired measure of potential. While I shall discuss the steps individually below, the basic technique I am reporting consists of a leap from the unemployment rate to potential output rather than a series of steps involving the several underlying factors. Strictly speaking, the leap requires the assumption that, whatever the influence of slack economic activity on average hours, labor-force participation, and manhour productivity, the magnitudes of all these effects are related to the unemployment rate. With this assumption, the unemployment rate can be viewed as a proxy variable for all the ways in which output is affected by idle resources. The measurement of potential output then is simplified into an estimate of how much output is depressed by unemployment in excess of 4 percent.

THE ESTIMATES

Even though the rate of unemployment has changed through time and even though the economy has not experienced an unemployment rate as low as 4 percent since the mid-1950s, we can make some reasonable statistical judgments about the hypothetical path of output at a constant 4-percent unemployment rate. Our estimates are based on the relationship between the actual path of real gross national product through time and the accompanying movements in the unemployment rate. It is not surprising that we find the unemployment rate declining in periods when output is rising rapidly. And we find the unemployment rate rising when real GNP declines. We also experience a rising unemployment rate typically when output is constant, since the growth through time of productivity and of the labor force reduces the fraction of the civilian labor force needed to produce the same output.

These qualitative relationships can be turned into numerical estimates by standard statistical techniques. The data for the past decade indicate:

1. A rise in real GNP of about 3½ percent per year—nearly 1 percent a quarter—is required merely to keep the unemployment rate constant over time.

2. At a given time, each extra 1 percent of real GNP means a decrement, on the average, of about one-third of a percentage point in the unemployment rate. Thus, when the unemployment rate is 5 percent, we estimate that an addition of 3 percent in real GNP would have been required to yield a 4-percent unemployment rate.

It should be emphasized that these are average and approximate, rather than exact, relationships. Indeed, they suggest two different rules for estimating potential GNP and, hence, the gap between potential and actual. One rule calls for a 3½-percent trend line to represent potential GNP; the data suggest that this line can be anchored at the level of actual output in mid-1955, when the unemployment rate was in fact very close to 4 percent. The gap is then the distance between that potential line and the actual level of real GNP. The other rule says: subtract 4 percent from the actual unemployment rate (U); then triple that remainder $(U - .04)$ and multiply the result by actual GNP expressed in billions of dollars. If you have followed instructions, you now have an estimate of the gap. To put it into a formula:

$$\text{Gap} = 3 \cdot (U - .04) \cdot \text{actual GNP (in billions of dollars)}$$

Potential GNP is, of course, the sum of the gap and actual GNP. The two rules agree reasonably well, but they occasionally show differences that are not negligible. The smooth path of potential GNP generated by the 3½-percent trend line usually makes more sense when differences arise. Hence, this path is illustrated in the accompanying figure.

THE STEPS

The findings above assert that a reduction in unemployment, measured as a percentage of the labor force, is associated with a much larger than proportionate change in output. To appraise and evaluate this finding, it is necessary to inspect the steps which were leaped over in the statistical relationships between output and unemployment. Clearly, the simple addition of 1 percent of a given labor force to the ranks of the employed would increase employment by only slightly more than 1 percent: $\frac{100}{100 - U}$ percent to be exact. If the workweek and productivity were unchanged, the increment to output would be only that 1+ percent. The 3-percent result implies that considerable output gains in a period of rising utilization rates must stem from one or all of the following: induced increases in the size of the labor force, longer average weekly hours, and greater productivity.

Labor-force Size · Participation in the labor force as we measure it consists of either having a job or actively seeking a job. The resulting measures of labor force are not pure reflections of supply; they are affected by job availability. In a slack labor market, people without a job may give up when they are convinced that jobhunting is a hopeless pursuit. They then may be viewed as having left the labor force though they stand ready and eager to work. Furthermore, there are secondary or passive members of the labor force who will not actively seek employment but would accept gainful employment if a job came looking for them. This latter group suffers little or no personal hardship in not having work, but the output they would contribute in a fully employed economy is a relevant part of the nation's potential GNP.

There may be induced changes in the labor force in the opposite direction: e.g., the loss of a job by the breadwinner of a family might increase the measured labor force by leading his wife and teen-age children to seek work. The prewar literature debated the probable net effects of these opposing influences on participation rates. However, the postwar record has convincingly delivered the verdict that a weak labor market depresses the size of the labor force.

The Workweek · A weak labor market also shortens the workweek by creating more part-time employment and reduced overtime. Taking into account the normal secular decline in hours worked per man, there is a clear relationship between movements in average hours and in output. When output has been rising rapidly, average hours have expanded—or, at least, have not contracted. On the other hand, periods of low growth or decline in GNP mean more rapid declines in average hours per man.

Gross National Product, Actual and Potential, and the Unemployment Rate

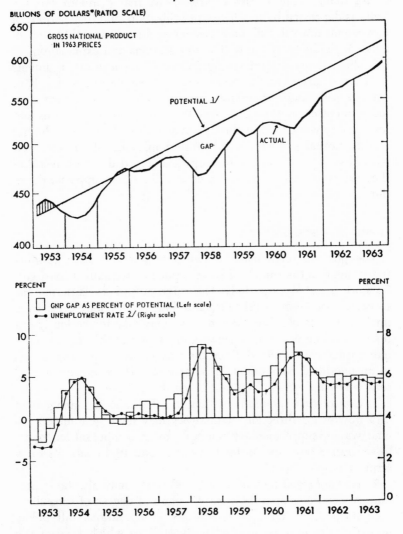

* Seasonally adjusted annual rates.
1 3½ percent trend line through the middle of 1955.
2 Unemployment as a percent of the civilian labor force; seasonally adjusted.
SOURCES: Department of Commerce, Department of Labor, Council of Economic Advisers.

Productivity · The record clearly shows that manhour productivity is depressed by low levels of utilization, and that periods of movement toward full employment yield considerably above-average productivity gains. The implications and explanations of this phenomenon are intriguing. Indeed, many *a priori* arguments have been made for the reverse view—that depressed levels of activity will stimulate productivity through pressure on management to cut costs, through a weeding-out of inefficient firms and low quality workers, and through availability of more and higher quality capital per worker for those employees who retain their jobs. If such effects exist, the empirical record demonstrates that they are swamped by other forces working in the opposite direction.

LABOR AS A FIXED COST

The positive relationship between output and labor productivity suggests that much of labor input is essentially a fixed cost for fairly substantial periods. Thus high output levels permit the spreading of labor overheads, and low production levels raise unit fixed costs of labor. At times, we may take too seriously our textbook examples which view labor as a variable factor, with only capital costs as fixed. Even the most casual empiricism points to an overhead component in labor costs. There are many reasons why employment may not be easily variable:

1. *Contractual commitments* may tie the hand of management in a downward direction—employees may have guaranteed annual wages, supplementary unemployment compensation, rights to severance pay, and so forth, as well as actual contracts for a term of employment.

2. *Technological factors*, in a broad sense, may also be important. A firm plans on a division of labor and degree of specialization attuned to "normal" operations. If operations fall below normal, there may be marked indivisibilities which prevent the firm from curtailing its employment of specialists, clerical and sales personnel, and supervisors at the same rate as its output. In particular, where there are idle plants and machines, labor is needed merely to maintain the excess capacity and keep it available on a standby basis.

3. *Transactions costs* associated with laying off labor and

then, in the future, doing new hiring may be another influence retarding the adjustment of labor input to fluctuations in sales and output.

4. *Acquired skills* that existing employees have learned on the job may make them particularly valuable to the firm so that it pays to stockpile underemployed labor rather than run the risk of having to hire untrained men when business conditions improve.

5. *Morale factors* may also make layoffs undesirable.

All of these factors could help explain why slack economic activity is accompanied by "on-the-job underemployment," reflected in depressed levels of manhour productivity. Firms obviously do lay off labor in recession but they do so reluctantly. Their problems may be mitigated, in part, by the presence of voluntary quits which permit a downward adjustment of employment without layoffs. In part, the impact of slack on manhour productivity may be reduced by shortening average hours to spread the work and the wage-bill without a cut in employment. But these appear to be only partial offsets.

Thus far, I have ignored the dependence of labor productivity on plant and equipment capacity. The entire discussion of potential output in this paper has, in effect, assumed that idle labor is a satisfactory measure of all idle resources. In fact, measures of excess capacity in industrial plant and equipment do show a close relationship to unemployment—idle men are accompanied by idle machines. But the correlation is not perfect and operating rates in industry should be considered along with employment data as an indicator of the gap between potential and actual output. Obviously, if capital were fully employed while there was much unemployed labor, this would hold down the productivity gains that could be obtained through full employment of labor. Robert Solow did use capital-stock data together with unemployment data in fitting a production function for 1929 to date. His estimates of potential output for the post-Korean period agreed remarkably well with those I am reporting.

IN SUMMARY

Still, I shall feel much more satisfied with the estimate of potential output when data and analysis have advanced to the point where the estimate can proceed step by step and where the capital factor can explicitly be taken into account. Meanwhile, the measure of potential must be used with care and any specific figure must be understood as the center of a range of plausible estimates. But the general picture emerging from the analysis of potential GNP and the gap is clear.

In the first place, it reminds us that the economy loses ground if it stands still. Unless the growth of output keeps pace with our ever-expanding potential, the unemployment rate tends to rise. The nation needs continually to set new records in production and sales. Its economy needs to grow bigger and better than ever before—because its labor force, capital stock, technology, and managerial and organizational resources are always getting bigger and better.

Second, the gap analysis points out that measures of unemployment understate the economic cost and the economic problem of a slack economy. The unemployment rate misses the submerged part of the iceberg associated with depressed rates of participation in the labor force, the shrinkage of the workweek through part-time jobs and the loss of overtime, and the sag in labor productivity. Thus, if we are to meet our targets of full utilization, we need expansionary measures that are large in relation to excess unemployment. According to the estimates above, the demand for goods and services must rise relatively about three times as much as we can expect unemployment to fall.

Finally, we can recognize that excessive unemployment has been associated with a tremendous economic cost since 1957. The figure above indicates that the United States could have produced a total of nearly $200 billion more output from 1958 to 1963, if demand had been maintained at levels consistent with a 4-percent unemployment rate. This is two-thirds of the amount spent for national defense in the period and far more than the expenditure for public education. It is fair to conclude that tolerance of idle resources has been America's outstanding extravagance and waste in recent years.

Dimensions of the Employment Problem

ALBERT REES

Albert Rees, professor of economics at the University of Chicago, was a member of President Kennedy's Committee to Appraise Employment and Unemployment Statistics. He delivered this address to the American Bankers Association Symposium on Employment in February 1964.

THE PROSPERITY of the American economy during the past three years has distracted attention from the seriousness of the unemployment problem. Yet there can be no doubt that the problem is serious, both in terms of the economic waste involved in unemployed resources and in terms of the hardships suffered by many unemployed workers and their families.

To assess the magnitude of the problem, it will be helpful to look first at the meaning of the term "unemployment." In nontechnical language, a person is considered unemployed in a particular week if he did not have paid work at all during that week and was looking for work or was a layoff. How good is this definition, and how good are the methods by which we implement it? To answer these questions, President Kennedy in November 1961 appointed a Committee to Appraise Employment and Unemployment Statistics, under the chairmanship of Professor R. A. Gordon. This committee examined with care our official definition of unemployment and our methods of collecting data. In its unanimous report, it made many detailed suggestions for the improvement of employment and unemployment statistics. Nevertheless, it concluded that "the concept of unemployment now in official use is a reasonable one and represents a conscientious and well designed effort over a long period of time to resolve a wide range of difficult issues." As a member of the committee, I concurred in this view. Our unemployment statistics, though they are not and cannot be perfect, are generally adequate as guides for public policy, and particularly for monetary and fiscal policy.

The concept of unemployment involves the notion of an obligation on the part of the unemployed person to make reasonable effort on his own behalf. The count of the unemployed, nevertheless, includes some people who are "voluntarily" unemployed in the sense that for personal reasons they are not actively, much less energetically, seeking work. No one knows just how many such people are counted. However, there is good reason to believe that these cases occur largely among women and teen-agers, and seldom among adult men, whose unemployment rate has also been very high in recent years by comparison with earlier periods. There is no reason to think that this so-called voluntary unemployment has been increasing. Finally, the existence of such cases does not imply that our statistics overestimate unemployment, for there are offsetting sources of error. For example, many nonworkers are not looking for work because they have become discouraged by repeated failure. Most of these are counted as not in the labor force, but they might, for many reasons, be considered unemployed, since an increase in demand could bring them back into the labor market. Again, no one knows how many such people there are in this category, though it is possible to make rough estimates.

The unemployment rates of the past six years have been high both by historical standards and by comparison with most other industrial countries of the Free World. In 1963, the average rate of unemployment was 5.7 percent, and it has not been below 5.5 percent in any year since 1957. However, the rate in the years 1955–57 averaged only 4.0 percent, though methods of measurement have not changed in any essential respect; and the years 1955–57 were no further from being peacetime years than those that have followed them.

By comparison with other countries, the recent record is far worse. In 1960, our unemployment rate was 5.6 percent. After adjusting foreign statistics to make them conform to our definitions, we find that the unemployment rate in Italy was 4.3 percent in 1960, in Great Britain 2.4 percent, in France 1.9 percent, in Japan 1.1 percent, and in West Germany 1.0 percent. Only Canada, with a rate of 7.0 percent, had a bleaker picture than our own.

It is not possible for the United States to achieve unemployment rates as low as those of Western Europe or Japan, because our labor force is much more mobile than theirs, and a certain amount of unemployment is inevitably associated with mobility. But it is possible at present for us to reach an unemployment level in the neighborhood of 4 percent, for we have reached it before during peacetime and without an unacceptable rate of price inflation. Many sophisticated criteria can be invoked in deciding what is a "satisfactory" level of unemployment, and no one number can adequately summarize our goals. In the end, no criterion seems superior to saying that we should be able to do at least as well as the best performance we have so far attained. This is, I think, the best explanation of the choice of a 4 percent unemployment target. Demographic changes in the years ahead will make even a 4 percent rate increasingly difficult to attain.

TYPES OF UNEMPLOYMENT

Let me turn now to the hardest question raised by our unemployment problem—precisely why has unemployment been so much higher in recent years? Is the increase caused by automation, by foreign competition, by tight money, by high taxes, or all of these, or other factors altogether? In dealing with these problems it will be useful to distinguish between three types of unemployment: frictional unemployment, structural unemployment, and unemployment caused by lack of aggregate demand. This last is sometimes called cyclical unemployment, a term which is misleading because it suggests a kind of unemployment that occurs only in business recessions. It should be understood that these are analytical types, and do not correspond precisely to any available statistical series.

By frictional unemployment, I shall mean unemployment caused by normal labor turnover—the time lost in finding the right vacant job when job vacancies are not scarce. By structural unemployment, I shall mean persistent unemployment caused by automation and other forms of technological change, by shifts in the composition of demand, and by the competition of imports with domestic production. I shall also include in structural unemployment any persistent unemployment due to changes in the structure of wages in relation to the pattern of labor demand.

FRICTIONAL UNEMPLOYMENT

Changes in the composition of the labor force could have caused frictional unemployment to rise since 1957. Different age and sex groups in the labor force have characteristically different levels of unemployment even when demand is strong. These differences in normal frictional unemployment arise from different mobility patterns. Teen-age workers always have higher unemployment rates than adults, since they are not so firmly attached to their jobs, and an increase in the proportion of teenagers in the labor force, therefore, raises the average unemployment rate. In other words, changes in labor force composition in and of themselves can raise or lower the unemployment rate as we usually measure it.

There have in fact been changes in labor force composition in recent years, but their net effect on the unemployment rate turns out to be negligible. The unemployment rate in 1962 was 5.6 percent. What would it have been if the composition of the labor force in 1962 had been identical with that of 1955, when the unemployment rate was only 4 percent? Applying the 1962 unemployment rates for detailed age and sex categories to the 1955 labor force, we obtain a calculated rate of 5.5 percent, only one-tenth of one percent below the actual rate.

The conclusion that changes in labor force composition play a negligible role in recent increases in unemployment rates does not mean that they will play no role in the years ahead. The rising proportion of teen-agers in the labor force, together with other projected changes in age and sex composition, will tend to raise unemployment rates slightly between now and 1970.

STRUCTURAL UNEMPLOYMENT

It is more difficult to assess the role of structural factors in our unemployment problem. Structural factors have been stressed by many observers because of the rapid spread of automation, a radically new technology in which the electronic computer plays a central role. Whereas earlier kinds of technological change tended to displace largely the least skilled workers—laborers and materials handlers, for example—automation and the computer are also displacing semi-skilled operatives in factories and refineries, and white-collar workers in business offices. At the same time, automation has created new occupations for educated and skilled people.

Although the new technology is highly labor saving and, at times, capital saving, the work done by the computer was not always done before by operatives or clerks. Often it is new work, which could not be done at all under older methods because it was prohibitively expensive. By lowering costs and thus expanding markets, automation can expand employment in some ways, even while contracting it in others. However, there is no assurance that the expansionary effects will predominate unless they are assisted by enough demand to absorb the output of an increasingly productive economy.

Whether high unemployment is primarily the result of structural change has been a cause for sharp disagreement, which is complicated by two sets of facts. First, unemployment has many kinds of structure: by industry, by occupation, by location and by education, to name but a few of the most important. Second, unemployment has always had a structure—that is, it has never been uniformly distributed even in periods of strong demand. The pertinent question for monetary and fiscal policy is not whether unemployment is concentrated in certain declining industries or occupations, but whether it is more concentrated than it used to be. The bulk of the evidence points to a negative answer. In particular, the structure of unemployment by major occupation and industry groups appears to have changed only in the ways that would be expected from the changes in the general level.

An example may clarify this point. When the general level of unemployment rises, the unemployment rate of operatives and kindred workers rises more than the average. It has done so from 1956 to 1962. But this rise could have been accurately predicted from the experience of 1946 to 1956. Those who argue that semiskilled workers are now being displaced by automation at an especially rapid rate should have expected a change in the relationship between the unemployment of operatives and of all workers—that the rise in the unemployment rate of operatives would be larger than the historical record predicted. It is, of course, possible that a finer breakdown of occupations and industries would reveal some structural change at a more detailed level.

Another kind of evidence lends strong support to the position that there has not been major structural change. The geographical dispersion of unemployment is now greater than it was immediately after World War II. There are still local pockets of severe unemployment, particularly in the Appalachian area, but such depressed areas now contain a smaller fraction of the total unemployed than they did about 15 years ago. We should recall the concern felt then for the depressed areas of New England, most of which are now no less prosperous than the country as a whole.

Hard-hit Groups: The Uneducated · Despite the fact that no major increase in structural unemployment is shown by data on industry, occupation and location, there have been changes in unemployment by education, by color, and by age. Professor Charles Killingsworth [1] has estimated changes in unemployment since 1950 by years of school completed and finds that workers who have completed one or more years of college have had a much smaller increase in unemployment than those with less schooling. The supply of college-trained workers has increased greatly, but the demand seems to have increased even more.

These changes could be the result of an increased demand for technical skills learned in college, so that, even with adequate demand, there would still be structural unemployment among the less educated and, at the same time, shortages of college-trained workers. This conclusion rests on the unstated assumption that college training is required for the work that college-educated workers do. This is often true as, for example, in engineering. In other cases, it is much less obvious. Universities, in hiring secretaries, will often state "college graduates preferred" and will exercise this preference if they have the chance, yet some of the best secretaries in my own university have only high school training and have learned academic jargon on the side, on the job. Employers use colleges as a source of training for employes, but they also use them as a screening device to sort out those who lack persistence, discipline and emotional stability. If there is an increase in demand, employers will have to do more of their own screening and training of workers with high school educations. This would avoid severe or persistent labor shortages in jobs for which college graduates are hired and at

1. See the following article.—*Editor.*

the same time reduce unemployment among those with less schooling.

Before we accept fully the idea that there are substantial shortages of educated people to offset the unemployment of the uneducated, we should note that data on the unemployment of professional and technical workers do not support the case for structural change. The unemployment rate of professional and technical workers rose from 1.0 percent in 1956 to 1.7 percent in 1962. While this rate is still much lower than that for the labor force as a whole, its rate of increase since 1956 has been greater.

Nonwhites · A second major change in unemployment in the postwar years has been the increasing unemployment rate of nonwhites. Although overall unemployment rates were about the same in 1949 and 1963, the nonwhite rate rose from 1.6 times the white rate in 1949 to 2.2 times in 1963. This change was largely completed by 1955.

In absolute terms, the rate of unemployment for nonwhites in 1963 was 11 percent. Detailed analysis shows that the rise in relative unemployment of nonwhites was not due to changes in occupational mix but has taken place within each major occupational group.

What is responsible for the rise in the relative unemployment rate of nonwhites? It seems unlikely, in the face of recent legislative and social changes, that this can reflect greater discrimination in employment since 1955 than before. Two factors may be responsible. Despite the increase in nonfarm employment opportunities for Negroes, the migration out of Southern agriculture may have increased the supply available even more. Second, the relative educational levels of nonwhites may be deteriorating not in the measurable sense of years of school completed, where the reverse is true, but in terms of quality. White populations are increasingly concentrated in suburbs with good educational systems, while nonwhites are increasingly concentrated in the slums of the large cities. There is much evidence that schools and teachers in urban slums are failing to overcome the barriers of environment and family indifference and thus failing to reach the minds, spur the ambitions or win the respect of their pupils.

Teen-agers · A final change in the pattern of unemployment has taken place largely within the past year: The unemployment rate of teen-agers—those 14 to 19 years old—has risen sharply relative to the rate for adults. The unemployment rate of teen-agers in 1963 was 15.6 percent, the highest level for any year since the beginning of this statistical series in 1947. Within the teen-age group, unemployment is highest for those with least education. In October 1961 the unemployment rate of June high school graduates not attending college was 17.9 percent; that of high school drop-outs was 26.8 percent.

The rise in teen-age unemployment seems to represent the conjunction of several forces. The number of teen-agers entering the labor force each year is growing rapidly. New techniques of production may increasingly require mature or experienced workers. Finally, union and social pressures are inducing employers to retrain or relocate present employes when they are displaced by technological change or plant closings, rather than replacing them with new ones. It is easy to understand why trade unions want their members retrained or relocated rather than discharged, and such programs are of great benefit to the workers involved. From another point of view, however, these programs may simply redistribute an inadequate number of jobs in such a way that young entrants to the labor force find it more difficult to gain a foothold.

About half of unemployed teen-agers are seeking only part-time work, and most are supported by their parents. However, this should not mislead us into thinking that youth unemployment is not a serious problem. Unemployment of teen-agers who are not in school is both an economic waste and a potentially explosive social force.

The increase in the unemployment of youth is a kind of structural change, but unemployed teen-agers are not structurally unemployed in the same sense as former coal miners or displaced packing house workers. They have not yet made a firm commitment to a locality or an occupation and are still a mobile, fluid resource like liquid capital. Thus an increase in demand will help reduce the unemployment of youth before it dries up pockets of unemployed older workers. Employers who hire experienced workers when they can get them will again train the inexperienced when they must.

Are Wages Responsible? · Before leaving the question of structural employment, let me touch briefly on another form of the structural argument. Some economists have suggested that the rise in unemployment among the unskilled, teen-agers and Negroes is caused not by changes in the demand for labor but by changes in wage structure. They argue that rising minimum wages set by legislation or collective bargaining have priced the unskilled out of the market. I would not deny the proposition that increasing minimum wages can reduce employment in the affected industries and, at times, increase unemployment. However, I see no convincing evidence that such forces have been important in our over-all unemployment problem. Legislated minimum wages, despite recent extensions of coverage, still are effective for only a small fraction of the labor force. The rest are either uncovered or receive more than the applicable legal minimum. The proportion of wage and salary workers covered by collective bargaining has not been rising since 1957—in fact, it has been declining somewhat—nor do wages in unionized sectors of the economy seem to have been rising relative to those elsewhere.

AGGREGATE DEMAND

What then of aggregate demand as a cause of our high level of unemployment? I have noted some ways in which it could be said that we have had an increase in structural unemployment. Yet structural factors will go only a small part of the way in explaining our present situation. We are left with lack of demand as the remaining and major cause of high unemployment. Consumers, businesses, and governments have not spent enough to absorb the output of a fully employed economy.

The Bottleneck in Labor Skills

CHARLES C. KILLINGSWORTH

When the Senate Subcommittee on Employment and Manpower, chaired by Senator Joseph Clark, conducted hearings in the fall of 1963, one expert witness was Charles C. Killingsworth, University Professor of Labor and Industrial Relations at Michigan State University. This selection is condensed from his testimony.

AUTOMATION, especially in its advanced forms, fundamentally changes the man-machine relation. Such a change is not unprecedented in economic history. The assembly line, as it replaced earlier techniques, helped to create literally millions of simple, repetitive jobs that could be learned in a few hours or a few days. Anybody who had two hands, two eyes, and a capacity to endure monotony could do the work.

The economic environment today is so different from that of 40 or 50 years ago that simply more of the same kinds of technological change that we experienced in the first half of the century would have a different impact now. But automation differs in some respects from most of the earlier technological changes.

One major difference is the much broader applicability of automation. The steam engine had a number of uses, but mainly in factories and in transportation. The cotton gin, the spinning jenny, the linotype, and others had a substantial impact, but each in only one industry. Computer technology in particular seems likely to invade almost every area of industrial activity.

A related difference is that automation appears to be spreading more rapidly than most major technological changes of the past. It is difficult if not impossible to measure the diffusion of technology in quantitative terms, of course. But I find these facts suggestive: About a century was required for the general adoption of the steam engine in those activities where it could be employed; the comparable timespan for electric power was about 50 years. The first automatic accounting systems were installed in banks some 7 or 8 years ago. Today, about half of the banks are in the process of converting to this system. When the first large-scale computers were introduced early in the 1950s, there were estimates that only about 10 or 15 of them would ever be needed in the entire United States. Today, nearly 4,000 fully transistorized computers are in use, and the number on order is about double that, so that in 2 or 3 years we will have about three times as many in use as we have today.

Today we have the electric eye, the iron hand, the tin ear, and the electronic brain. We also have the know-how to tie them together in self-regulating systems that can perform an enormous variety of jobs. There are two major results. One is a great reduction in the number of simple, repetitive jobs where all you need is your five senses and an untrained mind. The other result is a great increase in the number of jobs involved in designing, engineering, programming and administering these automatic production systems. Industry needs many more scientists, engineers, mathematicians, and other highly trained people, and many fewer blue-collar workers. Between 1957 and 1962 in manufacturing, production workers declined by nearly a million, while nonproduction workers increased by about a third of a million. The net change was a reduction of about 600,000 in employment.

Not all of the increase in white-collar employment in manufacturing was due to automation, of course, and not all of the newly hired employees were scientists and engineers. But the changing composition of employment was partly due to automation. Moreover, what happened from 1957 to 1962 was the continuation of a postwar trend in the ratio between production and nonproduction workers in manufacturing. Throughout the 1920's, the ratio fluctuated between narrow limits at around 19 or 20 percent. The great depression and World War II temporarily affected the ratio; at the outset of the depression, the blue-collar workers were laid off before the white-collar workers were, and in the war salesmen and clerks were drafted while blue-collar workers were added. By about 1951, the prewar ratio of about one white-collar worker to four blue-collar workers had been reestablished. But as automation gathered momentum during the 1950s, the ratio continued to change. It is now at about 26 percent and the trend is still strongly upward. Generally, the most highly automated industries have the highest ratio of white-collar workers. In chemicals and petroleum, for example, the ratio is 40 percent.

Let me preface my own analysis with a brief restatement of my argument to this point. The fundamental effect of automation on the labor market is to "twist" the pattern of demand—that is, it pushes down the demand for workers with little training while pushing up the demand for workers with large amounts of training. The shift from goods to services is a second major factor which twists the labor market in the same way. There are some low-skilled, blue-collar jobs in service-producing industries; but the most rapidly growing parts of the service sector are health care and education, both of which require a heavy preponderance of highly trained people.

I have already presented some figures showing the changing patterns of demand for labor. These changing patterns of demand would not create labor market imbalance, however, unless changes in the supply of labor lagged behind. We turn now to the figures which show that such a lag has in fact developed.

The table shows the relationship between rates of unemployment and levels of education of males 18 and over in 2 years—1950 and 1962.

Unemployment and Education, for Males, 18 and over,
April 1950 and March 1962

Years of school completed	Unemployment rates 1950	1962	Change 1950–62
0 to 7	8.4%	9.2%	+ 9.5%
8	6.6	7.5	+13.6
9 to 11	6.9	7.8	+13.0
12	4.6	4.8	+ 4.3
13 to 15	4.1	4.0	− 2.4
16 or more	2.2	1.4	−36.4
All groups	6.2	6.0	− 3.2

The overall unemployment rate was substantially the same in both years—6.2 percent in 1950 and 6.0 percent in 1962. But there was a redistribution of unemployment between these two years. The unemployment rates at the top of the educational attainment ladder went down, while the rates at the middle and lower rungs of the ladder went up substantially. The most significant figure in this table, I think, is the one showing the very large decrease in the unemployment rate of college graduates.

It is important to note that all of the improvement in the unemployment situation in 1962, as compared with 1950, was concentrated in the elite group of our labor force—the approximately 20 percent with college training. In all of the other categories, which have about 80 percent of the labor force, unemployment rates were substantially higher in 1962 than in 1950. These figures, I contend, substantiate the thesis that the patterns of demand for labor have been twisted faster than the patterns of supply have changed, and that as a result we had a substantially greater degree of labor market imbalance in 1962 than in 1950.

But these figures do not fully reveal the power of the labor market twist. The "labor force" enumeration includes (with minor exceptions) only those who say that they have jobs or that they have actively sought work in the week preceding the survey. Those who have been out of work so long that they have given up hope and are no longer "actively seeking" work—but who would take a job if one were available—are simply not counted either as unemployed or as a member of the labor force. The percentage of a given category of the total population that is "in the labor force" (under the foregoing definition) is expressed as the "labor force participation rate." It seems probable that worsening employment prospects for a particular group over a long period would force down the labor force participation rate —i.e., would squeeze a number of people out of the labor market altogether, in the sense that they would give up the continuing, active search for jobs. Conversely, it seems probable that improving employment prospects would tend to pull more people into the labor market and thus to raise the labor force participation rate. These two trends are indeed observable since 1950. The squeezing out of people at the lower end of the educational ladder and the pulling in of people at the upper end is another manifestation of the labor market twist.

Bear in mind that the unemployment rates for the lower educational attainment groups (those with 80 percent of the men) are now higher than in 1950, and that the unemployment rate for college graduates is now substantially lower than in 1950. Also bear in mind that the labor force participation rate figures strongly suggest a large and growing "reserve army"—which is not counted among the unemployed—at the lower educational levels, and that there is no evidence of any such reserve of college-trained men. Finally, bear in mind the differences between the lower end of the educational scale and the upper end in responsiveness to overall decreases in the unemployment rate.

When you put all of these considerations together, I believe that you are ineluctably led to the conclusion that long before we could get down to an overall unemployment rate as low as 4 percent, we would have a severe shortage of workers at the top of the educational ladder. This shortage would be a bottleneck to further expansion of employment. I cannot pinpoint the level at which the bottleneck would begin to seriously impede expansion; but it seems reasonable to believe that we could not get very far below a 5-percent overall unemployment level without hitting that bottleneck.

The Great Unemployment Fallacy

EDWIN L. DALE, JR.

Edwin L. Dale, Jr., is a Washington correspondent for The New York Times. *In this article, written for* The New Republic *in September 1964, he argues against structural explanations for the higher unemployment rates of recent years.*

IT SEEMS to this reporter after countless conversations with informed Americans—from intellectuals through bankers—that the country is gripped by a set of fallacies about the main problem of our economy and perhaps of our society—unemployment.

So deep is the conventional wisdom, and so pervasive through the right-to-left spectrum, that neither I nor anyone else has much hope of shaking it. But perhaps a try is worthwhile. Significantly, the one group that least accepts the conventional view is the economists, though they are not unanimous. The fallacy is in three parts:

1. Something new called automation (or "cybernation") has profoundly altered the conditions of production and employment in our society.
2. Jobs for the unskilled are disappearing.
3. These two factors, combined with the huge influx of teenagers into the labor market, present and impending, make the problem of curing unemployment almost insoluble—or in any case soluble only by wholly new measures of training or income transfer.

Given this set of beliefs, the sensitive American of either right or left simply cannot believe that such a measure as a general tax cut, or manipulation of monetary policy, could possibly cure the unemployment that he reads of or experiences. Yet it is the contention here that unemployment in the United States will steadily decline over the years ahead and that two or three years from now the great huzzah over automation and "structural unemployment" will be over and forgotten; that is, the conventional wisdom will have been shaken and abandoned.

My basic proposition will, of course, be recognized as familiar, if dubious, to those who accept the conventional wisdom. It is that general fiscal and monetary measures of government to expand total demand—and to maintain it when it reaches an adequate level—will *all by themselves* solve the unemployment problem. And by solve it I mean reduce unemployment, by our normal statistical definitions, to 3.5 percent or less of the labor force in two or three years. Such a level of unemployment is regarded by almost everyone as the equivalent of reasonably full employment. It means that the great bulk of the problem children of the conventional wisdom—the high school dropout, the railroad worker automated out of a job, the slum Negro—will have jobs.

Let me repeat, to be explicit: with no new training programs, with no shortening of the work week, with no special manpower policies, with no radical measures like paying people who do not work, this country will get full employment by expansion of demand alone. The expansion of demand will come partly by government measures such as the tax cut—that is, aggressive use, now, of budget deficits—and partly from a self-generating expansion of the economy fostered by the government measures. I can foresee only two possible reasons why the expansion of demand might be prevented: one would be the election of a too-conservative Administration, the other would be worsening of the balance-of-payments problem that would require a more restrictive government domestic policy. Neither counts as likely.

Before tackling the three fallacies, let us launch this argument with three true stories.

The first is World War II in the United States. Because of huge budget deficits (not because of the war, though the war caused the deficits), aggregate demand in the United States expanded enormously. Not only did full employment come rapidly after a whole decade of chronic unemployment, but employers quickly learned to train the allegedly unemployable. It wasn't only Rosy the Riveter but Stepinfetchit who got jobs.

The second is West Germany since 1948. For various reasons unnecessary to describe here, aggregate demand in Germany has been consistently high. The results, remarkably unknown in the United States, have been revealing.

Hordes of German refugees from the East and the South, most

originally badly located and many without skills, have all found jobs. The influx into the German labor force from this source during many of the past 15 years was greater proportionately than our present large labor force growth. In addition to the refugees, the movement off the farm in Germany was greater than here, and all these people got jobs, too.

Still the demand for labor was not satisfied. And so now half-literate *Turks* are being transported into Germany and quickly put to work. They are about as unskilled as it is possible to be, and they cannot even speak the language. Yet they all have jobs. This is to say nothing of Italians, Greeks, and Spaniards.

And to cap this story, the rate of "automation" in Germany has been consistently faster than ours, as measured by the annual rise in the output of each worker per hour or day or week. To-day, despite all these things, there is a severe labor shortage in Germany, with six vacancies for each unemployed worker.

The third story is West Virginia in the years from 1946 to 1953. Although the fact is little realized, the "automation" of the coal mines and some other industries was proceeding in those years, too. The total number of jobs in West Virginia was steady or declining. Yet there was no unemployment problem on the present scale. The reason was that the national economy was booming—because demand was high—and West Virginians got jobs in Ohio, Pennsylvania, and points north. These were years of full employment. West Virginia had a jobless rate a bit higher than the rest of the nation, but the state was hardly a "distressed area."

There is simply no explanation for these three stories except high aggregate demand. And they all reveal a crucial fact: if demand is high enough, the level of skills of the unemployed, or of the new entries into the labor force, is irrelevant. Employers take on the unskilled, and gladly, feeding them in at the bottom of the work-and-income scale. Perhaps the white soda jerk leaves for a better-paying job in the local factory and a Negro with six years education takes his place, but in any case the Negro gets a job.

Now a word about the fallacies themselves.

First automation. There is only one meaningful test of whether automation—a particularly advanced form of technology—repre-sents something new or only a continuation of the long process of technological change. This is in the figures on productivity, or output per manhour. By displacing labor, machines make the manhour output of the remaining workers larger.

Our productivity figures are not entirely satisfactory. But without going into a long statistical digression, it can be said that there is some evidence, still not conclusive, that our rate of productivity advance may now be *slightly* more rapid than it has been all through our industrial history. No more than that, and possibly not even that. It is simply mistaken to claim, on the evidence so far, that automation has meant a radical change. Some people, knowing all this, claim that it *will* do so, but this is really just crystal-ball gazing.

Note that I am not saying that automation does not displace workers. Of course it does. But so have machines for 150 years— sometimes outright layoff, more often less new hiring than would otherwise have been necessary. But whenever demand was high we have had full employment nonetheless.

Next, jobs for unskilled workers. This seems to me, in part, a case of the non-blind being unwilling to see.

In the last 48 hours I have seen the following unskilled people at work: street repairman, taxi driver, airport porter, elevator operator, drugstore counter girl, movie admissions taker, supermarket checkout girl, golf caddie, office boy, messenger, janitor, night watchman, garbage collector, building guard, cleaning woman, motel clerk, waiter, parking lot attendant, waitress, baseball groundskeeper, park cleaner. The only one of these that I can imagine might one day be automated out of a job is the elevator operator.

There is more to be said. The other day I was in an automated check-clearing department of a bank. It was impressive. But the strange thing was that nearly half the 25 jobs there (two more jobs than before the automation, though it is true that the department now does twice the volume of work) were, at best, semi-skilled. Girls were feeding checks through quick-photography machines, for example, and anyone with a good education would have gone crazy with the monotony after three days; these girls, as nearly as I could tell, were happy with the pay.

Obviously one cannot generalize from the particular in matters of this kind. But this is precisely what the "no jobs for the unskilled" school are doing—citing New York elevator operators or one or two other examples of that kind.

The fact is, surprisingly, that there is no evidence that unskilled jobs are disappearing at any faster rate than our people are being upgraded in education and skill, if they are disappearing at all. There is even some evidence, based on a breakdown of the unemployed figures, that the rate of unemployment among the unskilled is *lower*, in relation to the total unemployment rate, than it was ten years ago. I am not going to suggest that we will soon be confronted with a shortage of unskilled labor, but it is possible. Labor Secretary Willard Wirtz is right in urging young people to finish their education if they want high-paying jobs; but he is wrong in suggesting that those who don't will have no jobs at all. Not if we expand demand.

Finally, the growth of the labor force because of the teenage explosion.

One does not need the West German experience to refute this one. What about the decades of heavy immigration into the United States? What about the flood of Algerian refugees into France? The growth of the labor force is, of course, an opportunity, not a problem. In the classic circle of consumption and production, the worker in effect buys his own output. If aggregate demand is high—made that way in the first instance in our present case by government policy—the demand for labor will be high. It always has been and there is no evidence that the dynamics of a capitalist or market economy have so changed as to make this untrue in the future. What the labor force growth means is that our aggregate demand must grow a bit more rapidly to maintain full employment; and it will do so largely by itself if government demand measures are reasonably close to the mark.

So much for the case. Obviously only events can say whether the current conventional wisdom is, in fact, badly out of line with reality. But one can hope at least, that as the unemployment percentage drifts lower—now that we are actively using government measures to increase and maintain demand—the present fears about automation, the teenagers, structural unemployment, and the unskilled will die away. For if one must worry, it is better to worry about something real.

PART TWO

The Balance of Employment
and Price Stability

National Economic Goals

COMMISSION ON MONEY AND CREDIT

*The Commission on Money and Credit was a distinguished group
of Americans from the fields of banking, business, government,
labor and the professions. With the aid of scholars and experts,
they examined and evaluated the U. S. monetary and financial
system. This selection is from their comprehensive report, issued
in 1961.*

AN ADEQUATE rate of economic growth, sustained high levels of
production and employment, and reasonable stability of prices
are clearly the three objectives of central concern for monetary,
credit, and fiscal policies These three goals, however, must be
sought in the context of other important national objectives
which necessarily impose constraints on their pursuit. Among
such other objectives the provision of adequate national security
is of high priority. The maintenance of harmonious international
economic relations and contributions to economic development
abroad are also important. The Commission holds that a desirable degree of economic freedom and reliance on the market
mechanism for the allocation of products and resources is a continuing national objective. At the same time it recognizes the role
of government in providing a proper degree of useful goods and
services and of appropriate coordinating and regulatory functions. It is imperative also to preserve and strengthen workable
competition in the private enterprise system to assure the proper
functioning of the economy and the efficient use of resources in
response to market forces. And assurance of an equitable distribution of opportunity and income is important.

One responsibility of government is of special interest to the

Commission. The consensus reached and expressed in the Employment Act of 1946 is that:

It is the continuing policy and responsibility of the Federal Government to use all practicable means consistent with its needs and obligations and other essential considerations of national policy, with the assistance and cooperation of industry, agriculture, labor, and State and local governments, to coordinate and utilize all its plans, functions, and resources for the purpose of creating and maintaining, in a manner calculated to foster and promote free competitive enterprise and the general welfare, conditions under which there will be afforded useful employment opportunities, including self-employment, for those able, willing, and seeking to work, and to promote maximum employment, production, and purchasing power.

This stated responsibility parallels that expressed by most advanced governments of the Western world. It is not an exclusive responsibility of the federal government but one that is shared with the private economy. The more fully this joint responsibility is met, the greater will be the health and vigor of the private enterprise system.

THE CENTRAL GOALS

Adequate economic growth, reasonable price stability, and low-level unemployment are equally important as long-term objectives. If one objective such as price stability were sought with utmost rigor, the sacrifice of other objectives such as low unemployment and growth might be so great that there would be general agreement that it had been pushed too far. From time to time, however, circumstances may force one objective to move ahead of the others. For example, rapid inflation might involve such costs that stabilizing the price level would be given top priority, and the possible costs in terms of unemployment and growth would be borne with little question. These black and white situations seldom occur, and in the more usual situation the task is to seek them all simultaneously and in reasonable degree.

The extent of compatibility among these goals will be greatly influenced by the measures used to achieve them. Some policies to advance a goal may serve their purpose at virtually no cost in terms of other ends. Other policies may clearly sacrifice one objective for the attainment of another. For example, a program to expand growth by improving efficiency may involve no sacrifice in current consumption.

Monetary, credit, and fiscal measures *alone* will not be able to achieve a satisfactory performance in terms of all three goals simultaneously if resources move too slowly from one use to another in response to shifts in demand and if some groups enjoy and exercise substantial market power to push up or to maintain prices or wages at unduly high levels. Under some conditions in the past, both here and abroad, reducing unemployment beyond some level has been achieved only at the cost of a rising price level. Correspondingly, restrictions on price increases beyond some point by tight monetary, credit, and fiscal policies have led to increased levels of unemployment and to restrictions on the growth of output.

REASONABLE PRICE STABILITY

The Commission's concern with reasonable price stability is directed primarily to the avoidance of sustained, moderate increases in the general price level and of rapid increases even of limited duration.

The fear of inflation and the desire for a dollar of stable purchasing power are widespread in this country and arise largely from the undesirable effects which are believed to result from inflation. The adverse consequences cited are many, and among the most frequently heard are the arbitrary and regressive changes in the distribution of wealth and income, a slowing down of growth resulting from the discouragement of savings, distortion and waste in the allocation of resources, reduced productive efficiency, a flight from the dollar, and the tendency of inflation to feed on itself and thus to become ever greater, leading eventually to complete collapse.

Most of the arguments on the harmful consequences of inflation have been derived from studies of the great wartime inflations and the hyperinflations of the past. There is no denial from any quarter that the consequences of such price-level increases are so disastrous and costly compared to measures to contain them that they must be avoided. Few believe that such an inflation is a real threat in this country. No explosive inflationary situations have occurred without the reckless behavior of governments through the extremely rapid creation of money. There is every reason to presume that the federal government will avoid the kind of excesses that lead to galloping inflation.

The arbitrary redistribution of real incomes and real wealth are matters of major concern in mild as well as severe inflations. These effects, however, are far less drastic in mild than in rapid inflations. Our national policy clearly should be to avoid even mild sustained increases in the price level so long as the cost in terms of other equally vital objectives is not excessive.

The prevention of inflation has nearly always been an important objective of domestic monetary policy if only because of its effects internally. The level of prices is of critical international importance as well. It is clear that if price levels rise in the United States relative to those abroad, our ability to sell goods in foreign markets will decrease. Our international competitive position will improve under conditions of reasonable price-level stability in the United States whenever prices abroad rise more than here. Of course, it is the relationships among the prices of individual products that move internationally that are important in such comparisons, and although they are influenced by the same factors leading to changes in the general price level, each is also affected separately by technological and other factors influencing its costs. If rapid gains in productivity in the manufacture of such commodities in the United States are to be of benefit in international competition, they must bring relatively lower prices.

LOW LEVELS OF UNEMPLOYMENT

By the Employment Act of 1946 the nation set high and stable levels of employment as an objective of national economic policy. The Commission uses instead "low levels of unemployment" in referring to the same objective, for the rate of unemployment is the central concern. This rate may rise at the same time as the number of workers employed is rising because the size of the labor force as a whole is increasing faster than employment. Such a situation is not a satisfactory achievement of the real purpose of the high-employment objective.

There are two main reasons for the continuous concern with

unemployment. One is its direct effect upon those who are unemployed; the second is its effect upon total output and its rate of growth.

The unemployed do not enjoy the benefits of prosperity. When the percentage of the civilian labor force unemployed is used as the measure of unemployment, we must not forget the actual numbers involved. With a civilian labor force of more than 70 million persons, each increase of 1 percentage point in the unemployment rate means a loss of jobs for more than 700,000 persons. For the unemployed, being without a job means not only a loss of income and hardship for the family but also a possible loss of self-respect, a sense of personal failure, and, at times, a loss of social standing in the community. In addition, unemployment represents a waste of productive resources.

There is no really satisfactory definition or precise measure of high-level employment or low-level unemployment. However, a working notion can be based on a decision that at some level of unemployment, which would vary from time to time with the structural and other characteristics of the labor market, to reduce unemployment by monetary or fiscal measures is not economically justified. The cost in terms of inflation of generating the aggregate demand needed to create enough job vacancies to achieve further reduction in unemployment would be excessive compared with the cost of achieving the same reduction of unemployment by other means.

The Commission believes that an appropriate target for low level unemployment to use as a guide for monetary, credit, and fiscal measures is one somewhere near the point where the number of unfilled vacancies is about the same as the number of unemployed. In those circumstances there would still be unemployment and there would also be unfilled vacancies. But both conditions could be relieved by measures to improve the functioning of labor markets and to increase the mobility of workers geographically and among jobs of different skills so as to reduce structural, seasonal, and frictional unemployment.

ECONOMIC GROWTH

Economic growth is a major American objective, not as an end in itself but because it is a means and a prerequisite for the attainment of economic and other fundamental goals. Economic growth makes it possible to improve the standards of living of our own and future generations and to help raise standards of living in other parts of the world. The dynamic adjustments required by technological advances are more easily made in an expanding economy; competing demands for higher income can be most easily reconciled if total output is expanding. Finally growth provides the challenges and the sense of achievement that distinguish a growing society from a stagnant society.

Withal, growth is but one goal among many, and at some point any further increase in the rate of economic growth may be obtainable only by an increasing sacrifice of other goals. The maintenance of a level of aggregate demand sufficient to achieve high-level employment will result in a substantial rate of growth. Whether this rate will be widely judged adequate is uncertain. Because the costs and benefits are not reducible to any common terms that permit their objective measurement and comparison, the Commission knows of no optimum cut-off point for the rate of growth. This point will depend significantly upon the means used to achieve greater growth. Although not satisfied with recent rates of growth, the Commission does not recommend the establishment of any specific rate of growth as a target.

RELATIONSHIPS AMONG THE THREE GOALS

Unemployment and Prices · The relationship between unemployment and changes in the price level is fairly well understood in a general and qualitative way. An increase in the demand for a given supply of labor tends to increase wages and prices in both organized and unorganized industries. In the absence of any important elements of market power, wages tend to rise faster when there are more unfilled job vacancies (demand for labor) relative to the amount of unemployment. There is no universally applicable guide indicating the amount of wage and price increase, if any, which is likely to be associated with a specified increase in demand for labor or how much unemployment, if any, is likely to be associated with a particular wage increase.

The amount of additional aggregate demand needed to create a given number of new jobs, and hence a given reduction in unemployment, tends to be greater as unemployment declines. At some high level of unemployment, perhaps 8 percent, there is almost no pressure exerted on wages from aggregate demand. An increase in demand which then opens up 100,000 new jobs will reduce unemployment by almost 100,000 because workers of almost every skill category will be available in almost every local area. If unemployment falls because of further growth of demand, labor surpluses will tend to disappear in those skill categories and geographical areas where unemployment was initially smallest. Still further increases in demand will result in labor shortages and pressures for wage increases in these areas and skill categories, even though substantial unemployment may exist elsewhere. Each further increase in aggregate demand will reduce unemployment and will give rise to consequent pressure for higher wages. It is reasonable to expect that when unemployment has been reduced to 4 percent the pressure for wage increases will be much greater than when unemployment was 6 percent, and that by the time unemployment has fallen to 2 percent, unfilled vacancies will be widespread and the demand for labor will bring strong pressure for wage increases.

If the number of unfilled job vacancies is about the same as the number of unemployed, then unemployment cannot be said to stem from inadequate aggregate demand. Rather the unemployment would be primarily structural, seasonal, and frictional in character. Under these circumstances there would still be many unemployed, and there would probably be some upward pressure on wages and prices. Such a situation constitutes an appropriate target of low-level unemployment for monetary, credit, and fiscal measures.

The remaining unemployment and upward price pressures could be eased by governmental measures to improve the functioning of labor and product markets. While the costs in terms of government expenditures of such measures might be substantial, it is preferable and probably less costly to bear them rather than to require policy makers to chose between the costs of rising prices or greater unemployment.

Neither the crude data for the years since 1952 when unemployment averaged nearly 5 percent and the Consumer Price Index rose at an average rate of 1.4 percent per year nor the more elaborate statistical studies of past relationships of prices and employment are a firm guide for the future. The underlying conditions and the complex of factors affecting the relationship are continuously changing. It does appear, however, that attempts to reduce the level of unemployment below 4 percent by stimulating aggregate demand through monetary, credit, and fiscal measures *alone* will result in an increase in the Consumer Price Index. Attempts to remove the last percent increase in the price index by dampening demand *alone* would probably lead to an unsatisfactorily high level of unemployment. If the only policy measures available were those relating to total demand, the alternatives would probably be a measure of persistent inflation or an unsatisfactory level of unemployment.

There are, however, many other measures for fighting inflation and reducing unemployment simultaneously. Among them are ways of improving the effectiveness of labor markets to reduce the amount of unemployment associated with a given amount of tightness in the labor market. The government could provide better information for matching men and jobs through an improved employment service, eliminate discrimination against particular groups of workers, provide retraining opportunities for workers displaced by technical change, and help move workers out of, or industry into, depressed areas. These measures should improve labor mobility and should reduce localized shortages of labor at a given level of unemployment. This would lessen inflationary pressure from wages.

Similarly labor unions and business could reduce unnecessary barriers to mobility and efficient production. Such impediments include racial, age, and religious discrimination, nontransferable pension and welfare accumulations, feather-bedding, restrictive trade practices, unduly long periods of apprenticeship, and restrictions on entry into certain trades. Other measures would aim at increasing the effectiveness of competition in product markets. A continued vigorous antitrust policy is desirable to encourage competition and to encourage great price flexibilities. A low tariff policy and minimum use of quotas are called for if the United States is to benefit from foreign competition.

Changes may also be possible in those government policies which prevent reductions in individual prices, such as farm price supports, some practices relating to stock-piling activities, and other procurement practices.

If monetary, credit, and fiscal measures are supplemented by these other measures, then reasonable stability of the price levels and a low level of unemployment can be achieved simultaneously.

Unemployment and Growth · The role of aggregate demand in promoting growth has been widely discussed in recent years. Some writers suggest that the rate of growth of output will increase automatically if the demand for goods and services grows at least as long as there is some unemployment. Others imply that the rate of growth is independent of the degree of utilization of the labor force and of available industrial capacity. These positions would appear to be extreme. While the level of demand has an important influence on the rate of growth, it cannot be controlled by merely affecting demand. . . .

In considering the relationship between the level of demand, the level of employment, and the rate of growth of output, it is desirable to distinguish between the short-run effect of a *change in the level* of unemployment and the effect of a *continuing difference in the average level* of unemployment. If the unemployment rate falls from 5½ to 4 percent as a result of an increase in demand, output will increase because more men are at work and fewer of them work part time, and because of greater utilization of plant capacity. As long as this lower level of unemployment is maintained, the *amount* of GNP will be higher year after year because of this lower rate of unemployment. The increase in the *rate of growth* of GNP from this source occurs only in the period in which the unemployment is being reduced.

In addition to the immediate gain in output from increasing employment of the existing labor force, there will be a further gain for several years from an increase in the size of the labor force. New workers will enter or re-enter the labor force because jobs have become readily available. Continued low unemployment also puts pressure on employers to hire women and older workers. These changes result in sustained increases in the rate of growth of the labor force; they are more than one-shot affairs and should increase the rate of growth of total output. Finally, continued high employment may reduce the pressure for a shorter workweek and thus help forestall a factor leading to a decrease in total manhours.

Prices and Growth · There is considerable dispute about the impact of price-level changes on the rate of growth. Some contend that inflation is by itself a stimulus to growth, others argue that inflation is an inevitable concomitant of growth, and still others assert that continued inflation will preclude sustained growth.

Those who maintain that rising prices as such stimulate growth do so on the ground that inflation makes borrowing more profitable, creates an optimistic climate for expansion, and reduces the financial risks of investment. Those who argue that inflation hinders growth maintain that it encourages wasteful, speculative activity, frees inefficient firms from the discipline of possible financial failure, curtails the volume of saving necessary for investment, and may bring on a recession and ultimately a major depression as a result of a collapse of speculative activity engendered by inflation. These two views represent different aspects of the same phenomenon. When carried far enough an optimistic spirit which encourages investment can be an invitation to wasteful speculation. If rising prices reduce financial risks and encourage investment, they may also relieve inefficient firms from the discipline of the prospect of financial failure.

The evidence covering a wide range of periods and many countries shows that with price increases from zero to 6 percent per year, there is no appreciable association between the rate of growth and the rate of price change. As a broad generality, countries with declining prices or with rates of price increase greater than 6 percent appear to have lower growth rates than those operating within those limits. . . .

Both general considerations and the empirical evidence lead to two conclusions. First, there is no basis for believing that inflation is needed to stimulate growth. Second, although every inflation does not lead to a speculative boom which collapses into a major depression, the risk of collapse is sufficiently real that we must strive to avoid the inflation. The last consideration suggests that rising prices in a general boom are a matter of particular concern.

The Commission concludes that all three goals—an adequate rate of economic growth, low levels of unemployment, and reasonable price stability—can be achieved simultaneously, and that they are fundamentally compatible if we do not expect the impossible for each. While conflicts may arise under certain conditions between reasonable price stability and low levels of unemployment, there are no conflicts between low levels of unemployment and economic growth, and between reasonable price stability and an adequate rate of economic growth. Moreover, monetary, credit, and fiscal measures to influence the level of demand are essential ingredients for the attainment of these goals, even though not sufficient by themselves. Both labor and management must cooperate to make our enterprise system work effectively. Other government measures are required to supplement monetary, credit, and fiscal measures.

The Commission believes that under such conditions an appropriate combination of both monetary, fiscal, credit, and other economic measures should resolve potential conflicts among goals when they arise, and lead to their attainment simultaneously.

The Case for High-pressure Economics

ALVIN H. HANSEN

Alvin H. Hansen is Lucius N. Littauer Professor (Emeritus) of Political Economy at Harvard University and is generally regarded as the dean of American Keynesian economists. This selection is taken from his book The American Economy, *published in 1957.*

THE AMERICAN ECONOMY has undergone a considerable remodeling during the last quarter-century. I begin with what I regard as by far the most important single factor. It is a new factor, never before experienced in American history. And it is this. We have not had a major depression since 1938. Nearly two decades without a serious downturn. We had, indeed, a minor dip in 1949 and again in 1954—light jolts but no serious depression. And we have had virtually continuous full employment since 1941. Now this is something distinctly new, and we would do well to take a good look at this strange and quite novel experience.

I repeat, we have had virtually full employment and booming prosperity for sixteen years. Past experience has been quite different. Throughout our history every eight or nine years we have experienced serious depression and widespread unemployment. Indeed our economy was for a hundred years the most violently fluctuating economy in the world. And in the 1930s we had prolonged depression and seemingly endless stagnation.

THE MISSING LINK: ADEQUATE DEMAND

What is the essence of the American economic revolution of the last fifteen years? The miracle of production? The economy already had that *potential* back in the thirties, though the steam was unfortunately lacking. Now, however, we have seen what the economy can do under the pressure of *adequate aggregate demand*. We now have acquired at least some confidence in the government's responsibility for the maintenance of prosperity

53

and full employment. When the British Conservative Government, under Churchill, announced its assumption of continuing
responsibility for high employment in 1944, that Act was
regarded as a new venture of government, and so indeed it
was. The Employment Act of 1946 set much the same goal
for the United States. But it was not until President Eisenhower's
statement with respect to the firm determination of his Administration to use the full powers of the government to prevent
depression that general bipartisan acceptance of this program
was achieved. It is indeed a revolution in men's thinking. And
this revolution is in no small part the result of the vigorous
economic controversies which have filled the pages of economic
journals, and from there spilled out into the public forums,
during the last two decades.

Now someone will say that the miracle of production which
we have witnessed during the upsurge of the last fifteen years
could never have occurred without the resourcefulness of private
enterprise, the technical know-how, the technological innovations, and the capital formation necessary to implement the
new technique. This is indeed unquestionably true, and it is a
fact that should be stressed again and again. Yet even with
respect to these factors it is important to note that the cause-
and-effect relations are closely intertwined. The government has
made a major contribution to ensure adequate aggregate demand. The upsurge related thereto has stimulated population
growth, which in turn has contributed to the upsurge. The war
and the postwar upsurge have served to stimulate new techniques, and these in turn reinforce the upsurge. And finally,
investment in new capital (together with corporate and individual savings to finance it) is a consequence, no less than a
cause, of a high and growing national income.

Thus the American economic revolution of the last quarter-
century constitutes a laboratory experiment in which the flow
of events has tested on a broad front the Keynesian diagnosis
and the Keynesian policies.

The problems of a highly developed economy are different,
as we have seen, from those of an economy in the earlier stages
of industrial development. The advanced industrial society, having attained a high level of technology together with entre-
preneurial know-how and worker skills, has equipped itself

with a vast accumulation of fixed capital. The underdeveloped economy is capital-poor; the advanced country is capital-rich.

No one will deny that the developed economies of Western Europe and North America have reached, after 150 years of technological progress and capital accumulation, a high level of productive capacity. These countries have, moreover, within them the seeds of continued growth. Yet the output of the United Kingdom fell far below her potential throughout the two interwar decades, and in the United States the economy performed disastrously below her capacity for more than a decade before Pearl Harbor. How long must an economy fail notoriously to perform before it is generally admitted that something is seriously lacking?

Now it was Keynes' central thesis that the element that was woefully lacking was *adequate aggregate demand*. The classicals had argued that all that was needed was technology and capital, that the economy itself would automatically generate adequate demand. The interwar experience in the United Kingdom and the deep depression in the United States demonstrated, as conclusively as facts can, that the classical thesis, whatever may have been true of the early days of capitalism, was no longer valid.

But facts convinced no one. Facts alone can never destroy a theory. As James B. Conant has aptly put it, men strive desperately "to modify an old idea to make it accord with new experiments." An outworn theory will not be abandoned until it has been superseded by a better one. "It takes," says Conant, "a new conceptual scheme to cause the abandonment of an old one." [1]

In his *General Theory of Employment, Interest and Money,* Keynes challenged the view that the modern economic system can be *depended* upon to make automatically the adjustments needed to ensure full use of productive resources. The thing that private enterprise can certainly do efficiently and well is to *produce*. The thing that it cannot be *depended* upon to do well is to ensure adequate aggregate demand.

Just as the decade before the Second World War deepened the conviction that the classicals were wrong, so the last fifteen

1. James B. Conant, *On Understanding Science,* Yale University Press, 1947, pp. 89, 90.

years have strengthened the conviction that Keynes was right with respect to his positive program. Governments throughout Western Europe, and in the United States, have on an unprecedented scale augmented aggregate demand beyond that generated by private enterprise. And all over the free world, but especially in the United States, we have witnessed what the economy can do when it is put under pressure. Government expenditures, government borrowing, government guarantees and lending operations, government policies in the area of social security, agriculture, public power, rural electrification, securities regulation, deposit insurance, and monetary, banking, and fiscal policies have provided much of the *fuel* needed for the full use of the productive capacity created by technology and capital accumulation.

THE PROBLEM OF INFLATION

Operating under pressure the American economy has performed a miracle. The output response to adequate aggregate demand has surprised everyone, and, what is to many still more surprising, it has not led to any such destructive inflation as was feared. Clearly we are not out of the woods in this matter, but the experience of recent years is reassuring. One thing at least is certain. Our economy is equipped with three powerful safeguards against peacetime inflation: (1) our prodigious capacity to increase production when under pressure; (2) our capacity, both corporate and individual, to save at high-income levels; (3) our demonstrated capacity at responsible fiscal and monetary management. There remains the problem of wages and collective bargaining. This requires, there can be no doubt, statesmanlike action. At all events, I think it is fair to say that experience thus far indicates that the alarmists may well have beaten the drums a little too loudly, and I am happy to note recently a little softer note in the discussion of this very important problem.

A high degree of stability in the value of money must be an important consideration of public policy. Yet we are, I fear, in considerable danger of making a fetish of rigid price stability. This fetish could easily become a serious obstacle to optimum growth and expansion. If we are going to be frightened away by every slight increase in prices, we are likely to fall far below the growth of which we are potentially capable.

We use the term "inflation" far too loosely. The word "inflation" is used to describe the astronomical price increases experienced by Germany after the First World War, and the same word is applied to the comparatively moderate increases in prices in American history. The phrase "inflationary pressures" has often become, I suggest, virtually synonymous with "expansionary forces." Brakes are thereby applied, and output is sacrificed to rigid price stability.

I should like to propose a new definition—one, I hope, which might have some operational value for monetary policy. I suggest that we need a new concept which I propose to call "pure inflation," and I propose to set this concept over against the concept of "price adjustments to output changes." "Pure inflation" (and I emphasize the word "pure"), I should say, is a condition in which prices rise without any appreciable increase in output.

Countries which have suffered in the past from the evils of inflation have typically experienced large price increases with no substantial increase in output. Indeed, in cases of hyperinflation, output has often actually decreased.

There are, to be sure, degrees of pure inflation. And I should like to suggest, to help clarify our thinking, the following general observation. I suggest that at no time in our history, nor indeed in that of any other country, can it be shown that price increases have injured the economy and the general welfare if in the period in question the increase in aggregate output has exceeded percentagewise the increase in prices.

Frederick Mills, of the National Bureau of Economic Research, surveying eighty years of cyclical movements in our history, has shown that, in periods of expansion, for every 1 percent increase in output we have had $8/10$ percent increase in prices—a 5 to 4 ratio. Professor Mills' short-run ratios of output increases to price increases might, of course, develop against the background either of a long-run downtrend in prices or a long-run uptrend.

I repeat, one does not encounter the condition of inflation in any meaningful sense so long as percentage increases in aggregate output exceed by some margin the percentage increases in the price level.

I should be prepared, in special circumstances, however, to go a bit farther. There are times when a tremendous forward push is urgently needed, when a choice has to be made between permitting a price increase substantially greater than my rule suggests or else foregoing the needed increase in aggregate output.

Consider, for example, the situation in 1946 after the removal of price and wage controls and the cut in wartime taxes. Having chosen to remove the main restraints on consumption (and I assume that political realism forbade any other choice), what then? The only way remaining to keep aggregate demand in check would have been drastic monetary restraint on investment. Would this have been desirable policy? I think not. A rapid transition to full peacetime production required massive investment in plant, equipment, and inventories to make good the accumulated shortages caused by the war. It was a choice of the lesser evil. It did indeed mean a price increase percentage-wise considerably greater than the increase in aggregate output. But the massive investment laid the groundwork for a large increase in output later and contributed greatly to the slowing-down of the price movement by 1948.

Following the Second World War we had, as we all know, a considerable price rise. There are those who regard this as simply due to war and postwar mismanagement. I cannot agree. Granted that the controls had to be removed and that taxes had to be cut—that, politically speaking, they could not be continued for a year or so longer—then I think it follows that some considerable price rise was inevitable. This is true because of the accumulated backlog of unfulfilled demand and of post-war shortages. The closets were empty, the shelves were bare; consumers' stocks and business inventories had to be replenished. Under these circumstances price stability could not have been achieved unless indeed we had been prepared to cut employment and income sufficiently to reduce demand to the level of the then available flow of consumers' goods. And a severe cut of this character would have been necessary even though there had been no widespread holdings of liquid savings, since people were quite prepared, in view of the backlog of demand for clothing, household furnishings, automobiles, etc., to spend all of their current income. Any net investment in excess of corporate net saving would under these circumstances have created inflationary pressures.

The path we chose was much to be preferred. It brought indeed a considerable rise in prices, but it gave us full employment and it stimulated a tremendous outpouring of goods which already by the middle of 1947 had drenched the inflationary fires.

Periods of rapid growth have usually also been periods of moderate price increases. In the usual case the price system tends to respond in this manner to rapid expansion. It is not probable that we can achieve in the next twenty years anything like the growth of which we are capable, without some moderate increases in wholesale and consumer prices.

Economists generally tend to exaggerate the evils of moderate price increases. The accumulated savings, it is said, are eaten into. Inflation, it is said, tends to eliminate the sturdy middle class, and it concentrates income in the hands of the lucky few.

These things have indeed always happened in the great astronomical inflations. And conclusions based on these undoubted facts are then erroneously applied to such price increases as we have experienced in the United States during the last half-century.

The alleged evils which are typically cited are, in fact, based on abstractions that have no relevance to conditions as we actually find them in the United States. We have indeed experienced a considerable price upheaval both in the first quarter and again in the second quarter of the current century. But private property continues firmly in the saddle. Savings per family (after correcting for price changes) are more than twice as large as in 1925. Urban home ownership has increased from 45 to 55 percent. Farm ownership has increased from 58 percent to 75 percent. The middle class is stronger than ever before in our history. There is less inequality in the distribution of income. Adjustments in social-security benefits can be made and have been made when price changes occur.

In this connection it is well to remember that nothing eats so dangerously into family savings as deflation and unemployment. On the other hand, even the considerable price increases we have had since the end of the Second World War have not wiped out family savings. According to the Home Loan Bank Board, the accumulated savings, per family, in life insurance, savings accounts, United States savings bonds, and savings and loan associations have risen from $2,500 in 1944 to $4,200 in 1954, an increase (after correction for consumer price changes) of 10 percent in real purchasing power. I do not say that we might not have done better had not the aftermath of the war brought the price increases. But I do say we have not suffered the serious effects on family savings that are so often quite irresponsibly alleged.

Thus I conclude that if in the pursuit of rigid price stability we permit, and even foster, a considerable amount of unemployment, we shall then fail to achieve the growth of which we are capable. If, fearful of short-run instability, we fail to place the economy under the pressure of an aggregate demand adequate to produce full employment, we shall not even discover what our potentialities for growth are. Under these circumstances we could gradually drift into a condition of stagnation.

The Case against High-pressure Economics

HENRY C. WALLICH

*Henry C. Wallich, who coined the phrase "high-pressure eco-
nomics," criticizes it in an article entitled "Postwar United States
Monetary Policy Appraised," which was written for the American
Assembly in 1958. Mr. Wallich is professor of economics at Yale
University and was a member of the Council of Economic Ad-
visers from 1959 to 1961.*

AGAINST THE SPECTRE of unemployment in a low-pressure economy, the defenders of [price stability] can raise the equally serious vision of inflation in an economy running at high pressure.
Unemployment hurts a limited number of people severely, but
for the most part temporarily. Inflation hurts large numbers,
usually less severely, but the damage done to savings and relative income position tends to be permanent. If inflation should
ultimately lead to severe depression we shall end up with the
worst of both worlds. Yet it must be conceded that the public
seems to enjoy most of the manifestations of inflation and, unlike
unemployment, does not regard it as an evil demanding immediate redress.

Finally, the partisans of [price stability] can argue that full
employment and growth are not indivisible. It is at least conceivable that an economy running at a slightly lower rate of
employment and output for a time may in the end enjoy the
same or a larger average rate of growth as would a high pressure economy. If a low pressure economy grows at the same
rate as a high pressure economy, it will not lose very much by
leaving an extra one or two percent of its labor force unused.
At an annual growth rate of four percent, the loss of output
from one percent unemployment will be the equivalent of three
months' growth. At this rate, the low pressure economy would
fall behind the high pressure economy only very little.

Whether or not the same rate of growth can be expected in
the two economies depends principally on the kind of pressure
prevailing in the high pressure system. It may be the kind that

results from high investment financed by bank credit, creating large profits and imposing "forced savings" on the consumer by preventing him from consuming as much as he would like. This kind of inflationary pressure probably accelerates growth, at least for a while. The inflationary pressure may also be of the type known as cost push, however. In that case, consumption rather than investment will be the expanding force. Whether growth can much accelerate in this type of situation is doubtful, and what will happen eventually if inflation should gain momentum or be brought to a sudden halt is quite obscure. The recent inflation in the United States has had many of the earmarks of cost-push inflation, although it has also featured an expansion of investment.

It is on the longer-run consequences of inflation that the defenders of stable prices must fundamentally rest their case. In the short run all sorts of good things can be promised and performed by the high pressure economy—fuller employment, more output, more growth. What will happen in the long run?

The United States has no experience of a prolonged inflation consciously felt as such. Prolonged upward price movements have occurred—from 1896 to 1940, or even from 1933 to the present. But when those who think inflation is relatively harmless point to these periods as evidence, they overlook one basic distinction: those price increases were not viewed by the public as a continuing process. An inflation that is expected to continue, one that everybody tries to stay ahead of, is a new phenomenon. Consequently, we cannot appeal to experience in trying to forecast the long-run results of inflation. We depend upon surmises. That is the great uncertainty in the debate over inflation.

It has been argued that permanent inflation must inevitably accelerate from a creep to a run. As its victims learn to defend themselves, by obtaining quicker wage and salary adjustment or through escalation, the beneficiaries must move their own demands ahead faster and faster to preserve their gains. Galloping inflation, however, is obviously unsustainable; it must end in collapse or it will be stopped in some other, probably drastic manner.

This chain of reasoning is plausible but not compelling. If inflation is fought vigorously, it may well be held to a permanent or intermittent creep. Perhaps the best one can say is that acceleration constitutes a serious risk.

But even if it does not accelerate, continuing inflation will, in the view of those who oppose it, do increasing harm. The distortion of investment decisions, the discouragement of saving, the compulsion to speculate, the misallocation of resources, the strengthening of the monopoly position of firms owning old and low cost equipment—all are familiar dangers that have been pointed out many times. The inherent instability of an economy in which everything is worth what it is only because it is expected to be worth more next year; the fluctuations in the value of "inflation hedges" produced by the uncertain speed of the inflation; the need to concentrate all efforts on staying ahead of the game—all this does not add up to a satisfactory picture of a stable and rapidly growing economy. And, as the moralistically inclined may feel tempted to add, a society in which all contracts and financial promises are made with the afterthought that they will be partly cancelled by inflation, does not offer a morally-elevating picture either.

Few of the critics of inflation would claim that they can foresee its ultimate consequences. It may lead to collapse into deep depression, or simply to more inflation with stagnating growth. Or more likely, it will lead to price controls imposed under the pressure of impatient citizens and politicians. The immediate sacrifices that a policy of stable prices demands seem preferable to any of these.

I have presented here what I believe to be the main points of view in the debate over the objectives of policy, a debate that has gained urgency ever since the recent boom seemed to open a chasm between the objectives of price stability on one side and growth and full employment on the other. In this debate, the inflationists enjoy one great advantage: in the short run, they are usually right. More can be got out of an economy over a few months or years by running it at high pressure instead of at low. The chickens take some time to come home to roost—if they do come.

The supporters of stable prices labor under a corresponding difficulty. Theirs is a long-run case, in a world where experience consists of a succession of short runs. At best they can argue that the period during which inflation may help growth has become shorter, because everybody is watching the price index.

Inflation anticipated holds fewer promises and far more threats than inflation noted only after the event. Their case could be proved only, if at all, over a prolonged period and at great ultimate cost. One may hope that this form of proof will never have to be supplied. But one must realize also that so long as it has not, the inflationists will always have a plausible argument.

The Threat of Inflationary Psychology

ARTHUR F. BURNS

Arthur F. Burns is John Bates Clark Professor of Economics at Columbia University and president of the National Bureau of Economic Research. From 1953 to 1956 he was chairman of the Council of Economic Advisers. This selection is condensed from an address entitled "Monetary Policy and the Threat of Inflation" delivered to the American Assembly in 1958.

THE ECONOMIC opportunities that are ahead of our nation are prodigious, provided we have the wisdom to make the most of them. The fear of stagnation, which inhibited progress during the 1930s, has left us. Our population is increasing rapidly and we know it is very likely to continue to do so. We know that our industrial plant is growing and improving abundantly. We know that research and development work has become one of our major industries, and that this effort is yielding a large and steadily increasing harvest of new and improved products, new and improved materials, and new and improved technical processes. We know that our investment opportunities are and will remain prolific as long as we have the incentive to exercise our imagination sufficiently to create them. We know that, as a people, we are more eager than ever to better ourselves and to raise the level on which we and our children live.

Our faith in the nation's economic future is based on this strong foundation of knowledge. Yet there are also clouds on the economic horizon, and the most ominous of them is inflation.

I need not dwell on the injustices of inflation. Inflation, even if it proceeds at a gentle pace, works hardships over the years on school teachers, civil servants, and many other millions of unorganized workers. It works hardships on the growing numbers whose livelihood depends on pensions or securities that bear a fixed return in dollars. It impairs the savings of people in every income group of our society, but especially the savings of people of modest incomes, who have neither the means nor the knowledge to arrange their investments so as to reduce or escape the toll of inflation.

These injustices of inflation are as obvious as they are serious. But continued inflation not only mars a nation's prosperity. It may also endanger it by striking more directly at its roots.

In the first place, inflation distorts the accounts of business firms and thereby creates at times an illusion of profits when in fact capital is being consumed. This is undoubtedly happening in some of our corporations.

In the second place, inflation reduces the nation's ability to sell in foreign markets. The recent loss of gold should serve to remind us that, while our stocks of gold remain very ample, it would be imprudent to assume that we will necessarily escape a balance-of-payments problem a few years from now.

In the third place, inflation is always apt to give rise to expectations of further inflation. Once such attitudes become widespread, extensive speculation in commodities, or real estate, or securities will inevitably occur and in time may lead to a general collapse of the economy. . . .

An inflationary psychology is spreading. It does not appear to be based on short-term expectations, but rather on judgments of what the long future may have in store for us.

The belief derives force not only from the broad history of money and prices since the 1930s. Unhappily, it derives force, also, from the behavior of federal finances, money, wages, and prices during the more recent past. Let me cite some salient facts.

First, the resistance of wages to declining business activity, which has always been present in some degree, has become much stronger in recent times. The average hourly earnings of labor in manufacturing industries declined 22 percent during the severe recession of 1920–21, but declined only 1 percent during the severe recession of 1937–38. Hourly earnings responded with small declines to the two mild recessions of the 1920s, but hardly budged during the recessions of 1948–49 and 1953–54. During our most recent recession, that of 1957–58, wages actually rose appreciably. . . .

If the price of labor rises energetically during periods of expanding business activity, as we know it commonly does, and if it fails to decline or even rises further during recessions, as it has of late, then it seems clear that wages are bound to exercise more or less steadily an upward push on prices, unless improvements in productivity become much larger than they have been in recent times.

When we turn next to prices, we find again a striking change from earlier patterns of behavior. Over a long stretch of our history, prices rose briskly in wholesale markets during most periods of expanding business activity but also declined briskly during most business slumps. In these circumstances it was natural to suppose, whenever any substantial advance of the price level occurred, that prices would drop materially during the next decline or two in business activity and, consequently, that no permanent deterioration would take place in the purchasing power of money.

In the light of the history of prices since the war, expectations of this sort would no longer seem reasonable. Thus, during the two full business cycles since 1949, the average level of wholesale prices rose 13 percent during the first expansion and 7 percent during the second, but declined only four-tenths of one percent during the recession of 1953–54 and actually rose 1 percent during the recession of 1957–58.

The behavior of consumer prices has been similar They rose on the average 13 percent during the expansion phase of the business cycle from 1949 to 1954 and another three-tenths of one percent during the contraction.

The emphasis will vary from one individual to another, but nowadays more and more people are making, and with considerable justification, several—if not all—of the following generalizations.

1. During periods when the demand for goods and services is rising, competition tends to raise both prices and wages.
2. During periods when the demand for goods and services is declining, trade unions generally have sufficient power to maintain wages and often even to raise them.
3. This tendency is reinforced by the growing practice of entering into labor agreements that call for higher wages or larger fringe benefits at future dates without regard to the state of employment or profits that may then exist.
4. The rigidity or upward push of wage rates during recessions leads to some rigidity or even advance on the part of prices.
5. Quite apart from this, many business firms—especially the

larger corporations—tend to compete increasingly on the basis of the type of product, its quality, and the services accompanying its sale, rather than on the basis of price.

6. The widening spread of consumer and mortgage credit is leading many consumers to pay less attention to prices and more to the size of monthly payments.

7. While prices in numerous markets remain flexible, there seems to be a tendency on the part of government to shelter producers, now in one industry then in another, from the forces of market competition.

8. Although both wages and prices would undoubtedly become flexible if a recession deepened into a protracted depression, it is now the established policy of our government to use all practicable means to moderate business declines and it may be confidently expected that this policy will prevail in the future.

9. While the government has in recent times repeatedly demonstrated a willingness and power to counteract the forces of recession, its approach to the problem of inflation has been both less imaginative and less enterprising, and there is as yet no persuasive evidence for expecting a different approach.

10. Finally, and as a consequence of the preceding generalizations, our nation faces a threat of inflation over the coming years and decades.

Most people expect the inflation to be of the gradual or creeping variety. Very few expect any runaway or galloping inflation to develop. But the state of people's expectations cannot be safely assumed to remain constant. As more and more individuals come to believe in the inevitability of a creeping inflation, there is always a danger that they will behave in ways that add powerfully to the momentum of inflation and thereby strike at the foundations of the nation's prosperity.

Fortunately, we still have time as a people—though by no means unlimited time—to arrest the growing belief in the inevitability of inflation and to organize our economic affairs so that faith in the integrity of the dollar may be re-established. We could go about this task in many different ways, but I would suggest that our efforts are most likely to meet with success if we take two general principles as our guide to action.

The first principle is that, just as the government and private citizens acted together to bring the recent recession to a halt, so also will joint action be needed to avert the threat of long-run inflation that faces our nation.

Second, just as the federal government coordinated various of its policies and programs to combat recession, so also will it be necessary to proceed on a wide front in coping with the problem of inflation.

What we need more than anything else at this juncture is a national declaration of purpose with regard to the level of prices that could have a moral force such as the Employment Act, which the Congress passed in 1946, already exercises with regard to our levels of production and employment. This could be most simply accomplished by including reasonable stability of the consumer price level among the objectives of the Employment Act which it "is the continuing policy and responsibility of the Federal government" to promote "with the assistance and cooperation of industry, agriculture, labor, and state and local governments."

Although such an amendment of the Employment Act would not of itself assure success in curbing inflation, any more than the provisions of the Act as it stands assure success in dealing with recession and unemployment, there is every likelihood that the effects of the amendment would prove wholesome. In the first place, once the Employment Act is amended, the President's Economic Reports to the Congress will need to give closer attention than they have to the outlook for prices and to the policies that are required to maintain over the years reasonable stability of the price level. The reports of the Joint Economic Committee of the Congress would naturally move in the same direction. Most important of all, a declaration by the Congress that it is the continuing policy of the federal government to promote stability of the price level, as well as maximum production, employment, and incomes, would put private groups on notice that the government is determined to protect the dollar against further encroachment, and that the paths which governmental policy takes will depend largely on the moderation that business managers practice with regard to prices and that trade union leaders observe with regard to wages.

I would urge an early amendment of the Employment Act,

so as to make stability of the consumer price level an explicit and solemn objective of national economic policy, because I believe that this is the most effective action that the government can now take to arrest the dangerously spreading belief that we are living in an age of inflation. But if the change in people's psychology is to prove permanent, other measures will need to follow. One of the most important needs is to reassert the primacy of consumers, which includes everyone, and to reduce the power that special groups have come to have in our economy. Three broad lines of action are, I think, both desirable and practical.

In the first place, we need to undertake an agonizing reappraisal of the patchwork of price supports, wage regulations, import duties, import quotas, stockpiles, and subsidies that our government has evolved through the years. Although some of this legislation is surely in the public interest, there can also be little doubt that the broad effect of it all is to raise prices or to prevent them from falling.

In the second place, we need to strengthen the anti-trust laws, especially with regard to the formation of new mergers, and also make more liberal budgetary provisions for enforcement.

Third, as far as trade unions are concerned, the least that we can do is to subject their finances, as well as the election of their officials, to standards defined by law. Although such legislation will have no direct effect on wage bargaining, it will serve to remind the leaders of trade unions that unless they practice greater restraint in the future, the government may need to take drastic steps to curb their power to push up costs and prices.

Our country began to make good progress in solving the problem of depressions only after we became sufficiently aroused to seek workable solutions. With this moral and economic achievement to our credit, it is reasonable to expect, once we become sufficiently aroused over what is happening to the dollar, that we will also make good progress toward the more difficult goal of Prosperity Without Inflation.

Our Menu of Policy Choices

PAUL A. SAMUELSON AND ROBERT M. SOLOW

Paul A. Samuelson and Robert M. Solow, both professors of economics at The Massachusetts Institute of Technology, presented a paper on anti-inflationary policy at the American Economic Association meetings in December 1959. In the following portion of the paper, they analyze the effects of unemployment levels on the rate of inflation.

CONSIDER THE QUESTION of the relation between money wage changes and the degree of unemployment. We have A. W. Phillips' interesting paper on British history since the Civil War (our Civil War, that is!). His findings are remarkable, even if one disagrees with his interpretations.

In the first place, the period 1861–1913, during which the trade-union movement was rather weak, shows a fairly close relationship between the percent change in wage rates and the fraction of the labor force unemployed. Due allowance must be made for sharp import-price-induced changes in the cost of living, and for the normal expectation that wages will be rising faster when an unemployment rate of 5 percent is reached on the upswing than when it is reached on the downswing. In the second place, with minor exceptions, the same relationship that fits for 1861–1913 also seems to fit about as well for 1913–48 and 1948–57. And finally Phillips concludes that the money wage level would stabilize with 5 percent unemployment; and the rate of increase of money wages would be held down to the 2–3 percent rate of productivity increase with about 2½ percent of the labor force unemployed.

In spite of all its deficiencies, we think the accompanying scatter diagram in Figure 1 is useful. Where it does not provide answers, it at least asks interesting questions. We have plotted the yearly percentage changes of average hourly earnings in manufacturing, including supplements, against the annual average percentage of the labor force unemployed.

The first defect to note is the different coverages represented

FIG. 1. *Phillips Scatter Diagram for the United States*

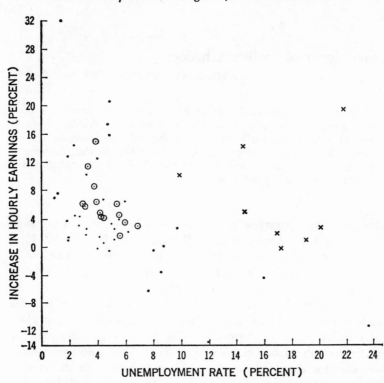

Points for 1933–1941 are indicated by X's; points for 1946–1959 are circled.

in the two axes. James S. Duesenberry has argued that postwar wage increases in manufacturing on the one hand and in trade, services, etc., on the other, may have quite different explanations: union power in manufacturing and simple excess demand in the other sectors. It is probably true that if we had an unemployment rate for manufacturing alone, it would be somewhat higher during the postwar years than the aggregate figure shown. Even if a qualitative statement like this held true over the whole period, the increasing weight of services in the total might still create a bias. Another defect is our use of annual increments and averages, when a full-scale study would have to look carefully into the nuances of timing.

A first look at the scatter is discouraging; there are points all over the place. But perhaps one can notice some systematic effects. In the first place, the years from 1933 to 1941 appear to be *sui generis:* money wages rose or failed to fall in the face of massive unemployment. One may attribute this to the workings of the New Deal (the 20 percent wage increase of 1934 must represent the NRA codes); or alternatively one could argue that by 1933 much of the unemployment had become structural, insulated from the functioning labor market, so that in effect the vertical axis ought to be moved over to the right. This would leave something more like the normal pattern. . . .

But the bulk of the observations—the period between the turn of the century and the first war, the decade between the end of that war and the Great Depression, and the most recent ten or twelve years—all show a rather consistent pattern. Wage rates do tend to rise when the labor market is tight, and the tighter the faster. What is most interesting is the strong suggestion that the relation, such as it is, has shifted upward slightly but noticeably in the forties and fifties. On the one hand, the first decade of the century and the twenties seem to fit the same pattern. Manufacturing wages seem to stabilize absolutely when 4 or 5 percent of the labor force is unemployed; and wage increases equal to the productivity increase of 2 to 3 percent per year is the normal pattern at about 3 percent unemployment.

On the other hand, from 1946 to the present, the pattern is fairly consistent and consistently different from the earlier period. The annual unemployment rate ranged only narrowly, from 2.5 percent in 1953 to 6.2 percent in 1958. Within that range, as might be expected, wages rose faster the lower the unemployment rate. But one would judge now that it would take more like 8 percent unemployment to keep money wages from rising. And they would rise at 2 to 3 percent per year with 5 or 6 percent of the labor force unemployed. . . .

Our own view will by now have become evident. When we translate the Phillips' diagram showing the American pattern of wage increase against degree of unemployment into a related diagram showing the different levels of unemployment that would be "needed" for each degree of price level change, we come out with guesses like the following:

1. In order to have wages increase at no more than the 2½ percent per annum characteristic of our productivity growth, the American economy would seem on the basis of twentieth-century and postwar experience to have to undergo something

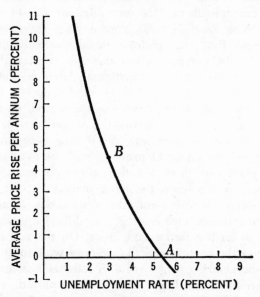

like 5 to 6 percent of the civilian labor force's being unemployed. That much unemployment would appear to be the cost of price stability in the years immediately ahead.

2. In order to achieve the nonperfectionist's goal of high enough output to give us no more than 3 percent unemployment, the price index might have to rise by as much as 4 to 5 percent per year. That much price rise would seem to be the necessary cost of high employment and production in the years immediately ahead.

All this is shown in our price-level modification of the Phillips curve, Figure 2. The point A, corresponding to price stability, is seen to involve about 5½ percent unemployment; whereas the point B, corresponding to 3 percent unemployment, is seen to involve a price rise of about 4½ percent per annum. We rather expect that the tug of war of politics will end us up in the next few years somewhere in between these selected points. We shall probably have some price rise and some excess unemployment.

Aside from the usual warning that these are simply our best guesses we must give another caution. All of our discussion has been phrased in short-run terms, dealing with what might happen in the next few years. It would be wrong, though, to think that our Figure 2 menu that relates obtainable price and unemployment behavior will maintain its same shape in the longer run. What we do in a policy way during the next few years might cause it to shift in a definite way.

Thus, it is conceivable that after a low-pressure economy had been produced, prices might continue to rise even though unemployment was considerable. Nevertheless, it might be that the low-pressure demand would so act upon wage and other expectations as to shift the curve downward in the longer run— so that over a decade, the economy might enjoy higher employment with price stability than our present-day estimate would indicate.

But also the opposite is conceivable. A low-pressure economy might build up within itself over the years larger and larger amounts of structural unemployment (the reverse of what happened from 1941 to 1953 as a result of strong war and postwar demands). The result would be an upward shift of our menu of choice, with more and more unemployment being needed just to keep prices stable.

Since we have no conclusive or suggestive evidence on these conflicting issues, we shall not attempt to give judgment on them. Instead we venture the reminder that, in the years just ahead, the level of attained growth will be highly correlated with the degree of full employment and high-capacity output.

But what about the longer run? If the per annum rate of technical progress were about the same in a low- and high-pressure economy, then the initial loss in output in going to the low-pressure state would never be made up; however, in relative terms, the initial gap would not grow but would remain constant as time goes by. If a low-pressure economy could succeed in improving the efficiency of our productive factors, some of the loss of growth might be gradually made up and could in long enough time even be more than wiped out. On the other hand, if such an economy produced class warfare and social conflict and depressed the level of research and technical progress, the loss in growth would be compounded in the long run.

A final disclaimer is in order. We have not here entered upon the important question of what feasible institutional reforms might be introduced to lessen the degree of disharmony between full employment and price stability. These could of course involve such wide-ranging issues as direct price and wage controls, antiunion and antitrust legislation, and a host of other measures hopefully designed to move the American Phillips' curves downward and to the left.

The Problems of Our Price Indexes

*Professor Richard Ruggles of Yale University argued in the
November 1961 issue of* Challenge *that our price indexes are
slanted—and hence so are our policies for price stability.*

THE BOGY of inflation is with us again. This cry, which was
chronic during the Fifties, has been a major factor in determining our monetary and fiscal policies. Since these policies are
based on the movements in the price indexes, it is time to consider whether our confidence in these indexes is justified.

Since 1948 the Consumer Price Index has increased by approximately 25 percent. A large part of this increase—about one-
third of it—occurred in the brief space of one year, at the beginning of the Korean war.

Let us take a look at the 12 percent increase in the Consumer
Price Index that has occurred since the Korean war. There are
major segments of consumer purchases for which prices have
not risen at all since that time. The price index for consumer
durables, for example, shows a decline of approximately three
percent. On the other hand, the index for medical care rose by
more than 30 percent. On the average, the prices of services
rose a substantial 23 percent, while those of commodities rose
only six percent.

This difference in behavior largely reflects the fact that the
price of a service is generally the rate of compensation of those
performing it. And these wages naturally rise as per capita income rises. In the last 50 years the prices of services relative to
those of commodities have risen continually as a consequence of
such general rises in living standards. Commodity prices, on the
other hand, can sometimes reflect increased productivity. If the
increase in output per man-hour is greater than the increase in
the wage rate, the cost of production may actually fall, thus
permitting lower commodity prices despite higher wages.

The identification of price indexes with rates of pay in the service industries involves the implicit assumption that the productivity of the service industries has remained unchanged. In some instances, this assumption may be correct, but in others quite wide of the mark.

In the case of medical care, for example, the apparent 30 percent price increase of the last eight years must be qualified by considering the increase in medical knowledge, better drugs and the new preventive medicines. Certainly the Salk vaccine was a tremendous medical advance which, in addition to sparing many lives, will save consumer dollars that would have gone for the treatment of polio.

Basically, then, the measurement of price changes comes down to a question of whether one gets more or less for his money. In the field of medical care it can be argued that most people would rather pay today's prices for today's medical care than yesterday's prices for yesterday's medical care. The fact that diseases were treated more cheaply in yesterday's world is more than offset by the increased knowledge and new drugs available for curing disease today. Although it is difficult to measure improvement in the *quality* of medicine in quantitative terms, there is no justification for ignoring it—which is what our present method of computing price indexes does.

The problem of measuring changes in quality also arises in the commodity components of the Consumer Price Index. In the Congressional hearings on government price statistics conducted early this year, Professor Zvi Griliches of the University of Chicago reported on the effect that changes in specifications had upon automobile prices. Dr. Griliches computed the value of specifications such as size, automatic transmission, horsepower, etc., by taking the price differences for a given year among cars with these varying specifications. Automobile prices were then adjusted to take into account the different features included as standard equipment in each year.

On this basis, using the value of specifications given by the 1954 price schedule, the prices of the "low-priced three" dropped 27 percent from 1954 to 1960, although their unadjusted list price rose 34 percent, and the Consumer Price Index for these automobiles reported a rise of 11 percent. The significance of this study is not that the Consumer Price Index for automobiles needs some minor adjustment to reflect the true price situation, but rather that the overemphasis on price change is itself in question.

This same kind of analysis could, of course, be applied to other major kinds of consumer durables, such as home laundry equipment, refrigerators and freezers, portable radios, cameras and hi-fi equipment. Almost all of these have shown considerable change in recent years. If the change in *quality* were taken into account the price index for consumer durables would have fallen far more than the three percent now reported.

Besides the quality change in existing goods, we should also take into account the effect of the introduction of totally new commodities upon the consumer's purchasing power. The index of consumer prices is purposely designed so that the introduction of new goods or the dropping of old ones will have no effect. Thus the introduction of such things as television, synthetic fibers and plastic products has had no effect upon the index.

But the introduction of new products obviously *does* have an influence upon consumers' standards of living, just as do quality improvements in existing products. It is quite possible to imagine an economic system which obtains its higher standard of living through the introduction of new products which are superior to the old ones they replace. In such a system, the consumer might continuously get more value for his dollar, even though the prices of the old products rose steadily due to rising wage and material costs. Yet conventional price indexes would show this situation as one in which prices are rising and consumers are getting less for their dollars. Although, of course, in our economy not all of the improvement in the standard of living comes about through the substitution of new products for old, it does seem clear that much of it has been achieved in this way, despite the systematic exclusion of this factor from price indexes.

Innovations and new products are not restricted to the durable goods field. They have, for instance, been highly significant in the food industry over the last decade. Meals are much easier to get and the choice available to the housewife is much greater.

It is, of course, not possible to measure accurately the dimensions of quality and product change. Nevertheless, one can safely suggest that, given the size of the average yearly increase in the Consumer Price Index since Korea, quality and product improvements may well have been much greater, so that we may actually have had declining rather than rising prices.

This does not mean that price indexes are completely invalid. Price indexes are useful in that they can show the relative differences in price behavior over time or between countries. For example, the eight percent increase in the price index at the beginning of the Korean war indicates that prices were rising more rapidly in this period than at any other time in the decade of the Fifties.

In periods of hyperinflation, such as have been experienced by some Latin American countries in recent years, where the price index may rise by as much as 80 percent in a single year, the indexes give a good indication of what is happening since such large increases cannot be offset by quality change. It is only in periods when price changes are relatively small that it becomes a serious error to use the indexes as an exact measure of what is taking place in the economy. In such periods the systematic biases of the price index may well be greater than the reported price change.

The defects of the Consumer Price Index are also inherent in the other price indexes which are used to deflate the gross national product to measure the change in real output.

In measuring the output of government, it is assumed—as it is throughout the service sector—that the productivity of civil servants never changes. The price indexes for this area are merely based on the changes in pay of government employees. While one may be tempted to agree with this evaluation of civil servants, the fact is that the introduction of computers, office machines and other automatic equipment has greatly increased the effectiveness of the individual worker. For example, the 1960 census data were processed by microfilming the original schedules and automatically producing magnetic tape for the electronic computers. Automatic equipment performed jobs which took thousands of clerks in previous censuses. Not only was the payroll reduced, but far more information was made available in a much shorter space of time. Output per census employee thus rose very considerably.

Similar examples of the increased output of government employees can be cited at the local level. For example, policemen have been provided with radio-equipped patrol cars and, more recently, transistorized walkie-talkies. Street cleaners have been given mechanized equipment. In some areas—education, for instance—progress is more difficult to measure. Yet most of us would be unwilling to have our children given the same education as we received, especially in the areas of sciences and mathematics.

In producers' durable equipment, once again, the price indexes leave out quality change and new products. But there are probably very few industries in which producers in 1960 would have been willing to buy 1950 models of machines even if they could get them at the 1950 prices. According to the Wholesale Price Index the 1960 price of producers' durable equipment was 23 percent above the 1950 price; if producers' durable equipment showed as much quality change as was shown in the study referred to above for automobiles, it seems probable that in fact prices actually fell.

For construction, both industrial and residential, the index is computed on the basis of wage rates and material costs. Thus again it is assumed that productivity does not change. While the construction industry is notorious for its lack of progressiveness, if we consider the new methods of off-the-site fabrication of components it is obvious that this assumption is not entirely valid.

Thus, we see that for almost every category of goods, whether purchased by consumers for household consumption, by government for public services or by producers for plant and equipment, the conventional price indexes do not reflect the effects of the introduction of new products and the improvement of existing products, or the increased productivity of those performing services. These omissions mean that the price indexes are higher than they should be. And since the indexes are used to deflate the value of current output and calculate its worth in noninflationary terms, our rate of growth is thus considerably understated.

It is interesting to speculate on what will happen to our measurement of output when further growth does not take the form of additional consumption of identical items, but rather of the consumption of goods of improved quality, the substitution of new products for old and the consumption of higher quality services. In such a world, our conventional price indexes would fail to catch the quality improvement; they would not recognize that the substitution of new products for old was any increase in the standard of living; and they would report the continued increase in the use of services solely in terms of the rates of re-muneration. Thus they might show an economy with constant output and rising prices, even though the standard of living was increasing rapidly. What is perhaps more serious, the conventional price and output indexes would fail completely to distinguish between a dynamic economy and one that was truly stagnant.

The single-minded pursuit of price stability, coupled with the false soundings given by our present price indicators, is likely to lead our economic policy makers astray. The tragedy of the postwar period is not so much the low rate of growth (which we cannot measure anyway), but rather the underutilization of our resources and the low level of investment to which the continuous existence of excess capacity leads.

At the quiver of a decimal point in the Consumer Price Index, the government has instituted restrictive monetary and fiscal policies. Its objective has been to restrain demand so that producers would find themselves with excess capacity and thus would not raise prices: and labor unions would be deterred by the existence of unemployment from seeking wage increases. The economy has been either in a depressed state or under restraining monetary and fiscal policies throughout almost the entire period since Korea. It is small wonder that in such an environment the rate of investment is low. In an economy where a false fear of inflation continually holds demand in check, even a low level of investment creates capacity which cannot be fully utilized. . . .

Computing the Consumer Price Index

EWAN CLAGUE

The United States Commissioner of Labor Statistics, Ewan Clague, has been responsible for the computation of the Consumer Price Index throughout the postwar years. He appraised the accuracy of the index in the May 1962 issue of Challenge, *reaching different conclusions from those of Professor Ruggles.*

IN 1951 a Congressional committee, appointed to investigate the Consumer Price Index (CPI), called it a "billion-dollar index" because of its widespread use in labor-management negotiations and in government policy making. However, there was criticism from certain sources that the index was far too *low*. It was said that because quality deterioration and other factors in living costs were not reflected in the index, it failed to measure accurately the extent to which prices had risen during the Korean war. After 12 days of hearings, the committee expressed confidence in the CPI as an "excellent index."

Early in 1961, another Congressional committee held hearings on the price indexes of the federal government, including the CPI. These hearings were devoted to a consideration of a report by a special committee of experts appointed by the National Bureau of Economic Research at the request of the Bureau of the Budget. This committee expressed the opinion that the rise in the CPI in recent years may have been too great—that the index is now somewhat too *high* because inadequate allowance has been made for improvements in the quality of goods and services.

What can we at the Bureau of Labor Statistics say about these criticisms? The best approach, I believe, is to sketch the methods we use to compare prices when the goods and services measured are not comparable over a period of time, and to explain some of the knotty problems involved in the concept of quality.

First of all, an increase or decrease in package size or quantity, whether or not accompanied by a price change, presents few problems.

Those people with a sweet tooth will remember when five-cent candy bars were made smaller. At that time the CPI reflected the increased price, but more recently it has reflected decreases when some of the bars were enlarged to their original size. Numerous relatively simple problems not involving quality changes occur, particularly for foods and toiletries.

To approach the problem of quality change, let us look first at how quality improvements take place. The annual model changes made in the automobile industry offer a striking example. Changes in style, changes in equipment, changes in structural and engineering features, changes in safety characteristics and changes relating to convenience and comfort are introduced year by year.

The first problem we must tackle in measuring such changes is to decide which new model is most appropriate to compare with the old. Names are not always reliable guides, so our first step is to compare various features of the new models in order to select the one most nearly comparable to the model priced for the preceding year's index. The next step is to eliminate the price effect of the *quality* differences.

Here our problems really begin. When "extras" become standard equipment, as when directional signals were included in the price of a car, we can use an established retail price for adjustment. Similarly, the higher horsepower involved in the change-over from a six-cylinder to an eight-cylinder engine can be fully accounted for. With the assistance of producers, we have made price estimates for some additional structural features in the past several years.

A recent analysis of our automobile data showed that, on the average, we adjusted prices quoted by retail car dealers downward by $700 between 1937 and 1960 (at September, 1960, prices) to take account of quality changes.

No adjustment has been made from one model year to another for some differences, such as curved windshields and redesigned bumpers, that may or may not have a significant effect on prices. While some of these are undoubtedly quality changes, there are others that represent style changes and thus should be considered price changes.

Most changes cost money, but should adjustments be made for all of them fo index purposes? I find it hard to place even a subjective value on tail-fins, enlarged trunk space (frequently empty) and the hump in the middle of the floor—all of which seem to be gradually disappearing without lament. While we are not entirely satisfied with the accuracy of our measures for automobile prices, we doubt that a great degree of inaccuracy has been introduced into the CPI by a possibly incomplete account of quality change.

Quality improvements are also made available to the consumer through the introduction of new grades or varieties of items which continue to be available in the old form. We have seen many changes of this kind in textiles, with the development of man-made fibers and special finishes that impart special properties to existing fabrics.

Late in 1956, when dacron curtains were introduced, they cost about a dollar more, on the average, than rayon curtains. Since both were in the market at the same time, we used this differential as an estimate of the value of quality difference.

The market differential may overestimate or underestimate the value of change in quality. The total price difference may represent novelty value as well as the value of basic quality improvements. In other words, the consumer may be paying more than the quality improvement is worth, in which case our index would be too low.

On the other hand, the price differential between the old and new varieties may be reduced as a result of economies achieved in the production process. In this case, the price difference does not make adequate allowance for the quality improvement, and the index is too high.

This brings us to another way in which quality improvements are effected. Many small, internal quality improvements are made which cannot readily be measured, in terms of price. A better cement for the production of cement-process shoes or the use of a stronger thread in the shoulder of a man's undershirt are examples. The values of such changes are small in any one period or even any one year. Some of them we have been able to adjust for, but I am sure we have also missed others.

Another aspect of the quality problem is the appearance of items that did not even exist at an earlier period—such as the wonder drugs. There can be no doubt that these are a great boon to mankind. They have saved lives that would otherwise have been lost. How do you go about measuring, for a price index, the value of saving a life? I believe everyone would agree that advances of this kind either cannot or should not be measured in terms of price.

My comments up to this point indicate that we have made strong efforts to take quality improvements into account in making up the CPI. We agree, however, that there are some improvements we have not been able to measure. The question is, how important are they? Are they so great as to offset the rise in the index of one or two percent a year? In our judgment, the increase shown by the CPI over the past five or 10 years cannot be explained away in terms of quality improvement.

Some of our critics assume universal and widespread quality improvement. But this assumption ignores the other side of the coin—quality deterioration. Increased fares for public transportation, for example, have seldom been accompanied by increased service. In fact, curtailed schedules and increased travel time are characteristic of public transportation in many cities.

Also, what about maintenance and repairs of automobiles, household appliances, furniture, etc? The quality of workmanship for home repairs has been the subject of vigorous complaints by homeowners.

We have not found any way of taking such intangible quality deterioration into account in the CPI. So, for some items, we have not shown *enough* price increase.

Finally, there are large sectors of the index that have not been affected by significant quality changes in either direction over long periods of time. Haircuts and heating fuels are of the same quality they were five or 10 years ago. Many foods, such as fresh beef and pork, apples, oranges, potatoes, flour, sugar and eggs are essentially of the same quality they have been for many years. Such items, with little or no quality change, have important weight in the Consumer Price Index.

To summarize:

1. The Bureau of Labor Statistics makes allowances for those quality improvements that are measurable. Its current procedures were specifically designed to offset the effect of quality change in measuring price change.

2. Unmeasured improvements in some areas are offset to some extent by unmeasured deterioration in others.

3. Emphasis on problem areas should not lead us to ignore the many items in the index which are little affected by quality improvement over long periods.

4. The net effect on the index of the changes in quality (in either direction) that have not been measured is very small in the short run. Perhaps cumulated over a decade or more, the differences may be significant, but hardly enough to nullify the increase in the CPI of 24.3 percent since 1950, or even the 11.6 percent increase that has occurred since 1955.

PART THREE

Fiscal Policy:
Principles and Instruments

The Workings of the Multiplier
COUNCIL OF ECONOMIC ADVISERS

The Economic Report of the President for 1963 contained this exposition of the multiplier process following from tax reduction. It was part of the Annual Report of the Council of Economic Advisers, which then consisted of Walter W. Heller, chairman, and Gardner Ackley.

TAX REDUCTION will directly increase the disposable income and purchasing power of consumers and business, strengthen incentives and expectations, and raise the net returns on new capital investment. This will lead to initial increases in private consumption and investment expenditures. These increases in spending will set off a cumulative expansion, generating further increases in consumption and investment spending and a general rise in production, income, and employment. This process is discussed in some detail in this section.

INITIAL EFFECTS: CONSUMPTION

Effects on Disposable Income · The proposed reduction in personal income tax rates will directly add to the disposable income of households. In addition, the reduction in corporate tax rates will increase the after-tax profits of corporations as a result of which corporations may be expected to increase their dividend payments. The initial direct effect on the disposable income of households resulting from the entire program of tax reductions should be approximately $8½ billion, at current levels of income.

Consumer Response to Increase in Disposable Income · The

ratio of total consumption expenditures to total personal disposable income has in each recent calendar year fallen within the range of 92 to 94 percent. Although there are lags and irregularities from quarter to quarter or even year to year, the change in personal consumption expenditures has in the past, after a few quarters, averaged roughly 93 percent of any change in personal disposable income. On this basis, the initial addition to consumer expenditures associated with tax reductions would be on the order of $8 billion, although all would not be spent at once.

Additions to after-tax incomes resulting from tax reduction are likely to be spent in the same way as other additions to income. The largest part of the proposed tax reduction will be reflected in reduced withholding of taxes from wages and salaries, and therefore in larger wage and salary checks; thus, it will be indistinguishable from additional income arising from wage or salary increases, greater employment, or longer hours of work. Similarly, part of the reduced corporate taxes will be passed along to stockholders in increased dividend checks. Stockholders will not be able to identify the source of their additional dividends. Tax reduction dollars carry no identifying label, and there is no reason to expect recipients to treat them differently from other dollars.

Recent experience with tax reduction demonstrates clearly that additions to disposable income from this source are spent as completely as any other additions. Taxes were reduced by about $4.7 billion on May 1, 1948, retroactive to January 1, with resulting large refunds in mid-1949. Again taxes were cut, net, by about $6 billion, effective January 1, 1954, with further cuts later that year. The table shows that the percentage of disposable income spent by consumers remained within the normal range of quarterly fluctuation during the periods following the enactment of each of these tax reductions.

It is sometimes suggested that tax reductions which add only a few dollars to the weekly pay check of the typical worker would do little good even if the money was spent, since the amounts involved would not be large enough to permit major expenditures—say on washing machines or automobiles. Instead, the money would be "frittered away" on minor expenditures and would do little good for the economy. But all purchases lead to production which generates income and provides employment.

Personal Consumption Expenditures as a Percentage of Disposable Personal Income during Two Postwar Periods of Tax Reduction

1948–1949		1953–1955	
Quarter	Percent	Quarter	Percent
1948: I	97.3	1953: IV	91.5
II	94.0	1954: I	91.8
III	92.6	II	92.8
IV	93.2	III	93.0
1949: I	93.9	IV	93.2
II	95.2	1955: I	94.5
III	95.7	II	93.5

Based on seasonally adjusted data.

SOURCE: Department of Commerce.

Therefore, the purpose of tax reduction is achieved when the proceeds are spent on any kind of goods or services.

Actually, of course, tax reduction which expands take-home pay even by a relatively small amount each week or month may induce recipients to purchase durable goods or houses of higher quality, since the increased income would permit them to handle larger monthly installment payments. It may even induce a re-arrangement of expenditure patterns and thus bring about purchases of durable goods that would not otherwise be made.

INITIAL EFFECTS: INVESTMENT

Investment is a more volatile element than consumption in national expenditure. The timing and magnitude of its response to tax changes is less predictable. But a cut in tax rates on business income will stimulate spending on new plants and new machinery in two ways. First, it will strengthen investment incentives by increasing the after-tax profits that businessmen can expect to earn on new productive facilities. Second, it will add to the supply of internal funds, a large part of which is normally reinvested in the business. . . .

Since the largest part of business investment is made by corporations, the proposed cuts in the corporate income tax are especially significant. But investments of unincorporated businesses will also be encouraged by cuts in personal income tax rates, especially in the upper brackets. The impact of the 1963 proposals to reduce taxes on business will, of course, differ from company to company and industry to industry, depending in part on the adequacy of their internal funds and their levels of capacity utilization. Though the speed of response may vary, industry after industry will begin to feel pressure on its capital facilities and funds as markets for its products are expanded by the 1963 tax program.

Furthermore, there are many individual companies for which the supply of internal funds is a constraint on investment, and many others that do not have excess capacity. Moreover, it is estimated that some 70 percent of the investment in plant and equipment is for modernization and replacement rather than expansion, that is, it is designed to produce new or better products, or to reduce production costs rather than primarily to expand productive capacity. For this large segment of capital spending, the stronger inducement to invest provided by business tax changes will translate much more readily into actual purchases of plant and equipment.

As production expands and existing capacity is more fully utilized, business tax reductions will provide an even stronger stimulus to investment.

CUMULATIVE EXPANSION: THE CONSUMPTION MULTIPLIER

Tax reduction will start a process of cumulative expansion throughout the economy. If the economy is already undergoing slow expansion, this cumulative process will be superimposed upon it. The initial increases in spending will stimulate production and employment, generating additional incomes. The details and timing of this process will vary from industry to industry. The first impact may be to draw down inventories rather than to expand production. But as inventories are depleted, retailers will quickly expand orders. As manufacturers' sales rise in response and their own inventories of finished goods decline, they will activate idle production lines, hire additional workers, place orders for materials and components. Thus the expansion will spread to other industries, leading to further expansion of production, employment, and orders.

Expanded sales mean increased profits. Increased employment means greater wage and salary income. Each additional dollar's worth of gross production necessarily generates a dollar of additional gross income.

But expansion does not proceed without limit. A considerable fraction of the value of gross production is shared with governments or becomes part of corporate retained earnings and does not become part of consumers' after-tax income. Some of the increase goes to pay additional excise and other indirect business taxes. Typically, when GNP is rising toward potential, corporate profits increase by about one-fourth of the rise in GNP. But a substantial part of this increase in profits is absorbed by Federal and State corporate income taxes, and another part is ordinarily retained by the corporations. Only the remainder is passed on to the households in dividend payments. Part of the additional wage and salary incomes associated with added production is absorbed by higher social security contributions. At the same time, increased employment means a drop in payments for unemployment insurance benefits.

When all of these "leakages" are taken into account, a little less than two-thirds of an additional dollar of GNP finds its way into the before-tax incomes of consumers in the form of wages, dividends, and other incomes. Part is absorbed by personal taxes, Federal, State, and local. The increase in personal disposable income is 50 to 55 percent. Of this amount a small fraction— about 7 percent—is set aside in personal saving, and the remainder—about 93 percent—is spent on consumption, as indicated earlier. Thus, out of each additional dollar of GNP, initially generated by the tax cut, roughly half ends up as added consumption expenditure. But the process does not stop here.

The additional expenditure on consumption that is brought about by the rise in GNP generates, in its turn, further production, which generates additional incomes and consumption, and so on, in a continuous sequence of expansion which economists call the "multiplier process." The "multiplier" applicable to the initial increase in spending resulting from tax reduction, with account taken of the various leakages discussed above, works out to roughly 2. If we apply this multiplier only to the initial increase in consumption (about $8 billion), the total ultimate effect will be an increase in annual consumption—and in production (and GNP)—of roughly $16 billion. Lags in the process of expansion will spread this increase in GNP over time, but studies of the relationships between changes in disposable income, consumption, and production of consumer goods suggest that at least half of the total stimulus of an initial increase in disposable income is realized within 6 months of that increase.

CUMULATIVE EXPANSION: THE INVESTMENT RESPONSE

Tax reduction will also have important cumulative indirect effects on investment in inventories and in fixed productive facilities. These effects are much more difficult to predict than the induced effects on consumption.

Inventory Investment · The stocks of goods that businessmen wish to hold depend upon current and expected rates of sales and production and the volume of new and unfilled orders, as well as on price expectations and other factors. An expansion of aggregate demand can be expected to raise business inventory targets. Production for inventory will generate further increases in demand and income over and above the multiplier effects discussed above, and will in turn induce further increases in consumption spending.

Inventory investment is volatile, and induced inventory accumulation can add significantly to the expansionary effects of tax reduction within a few months. At the same time, it should be recognized that inventory investment is exceedingly difficult to forecast. As the increase in production and sales tapers off, stocks and the rate of inventory investment will be correspondingly adjusted.

Business Investment in Plant and Equipment · A tax reduction large enough to move the economy toward full employment will also stimulate business investment in plant and equipment. General economic expansion will reinforce the initial stimulus to investment of cuts in business taxes. In the first place, narrowing the gap between actual and potential output—now estimated at $30-40 billion—will increase the utilization of existing plant and equipment. As excess capacity declines, more and more businesses will feel increasing pressure to expand capacity. At the same time, increases in the volume of sales and in productivity will raise corporate profits—in absolute terms, relative to GNP, and as a rate of return on investment. Internal funds available for investment will rise, while at the same time higher rates of return on existing capital will cause businessmen to raise their estimates of returns on new investment. When investment incentives are strengthened by rising demand, internal funds are more consistently translated into increased investment than when markets are slack.

Residential Construction · The demand for housing depends on growth in the number of families, on the existing stock of houses, and on the cost and availability of mortgage credit. But housing demand also responds, to some extent, to changes in disposable income. Thus, tax reduction will have some direct effect on residential construction. And as production, employment, and income generally expand, the demand for new homes can be expected to increase further. This increase will, in turn, reinforce the other expansionary effects of tax reduction.

STATE AND LOCAL GOVERNMENT EXPENDITURES

State and local government units have found it difficult to finance the needed expansion of their activities. Given the present importance of income and sales taxes in State and local tax systems, government revenues at the State and local level expand automatically as GNP rises. The additional State-local revenues generated by economic expansion will assist these governments to meet their pressing needs. Moreover, since Federal tax liabilities are deductible under many State income tax laws, reduction in Federal tax rates will automatically generate some further addition to State-local tax revenues. Finally, a reduction in Federal taxes will enlarge the tax base available to State and local government units and may make it easier for them to raise rates or impose new taxes.

Undoubtedly, some of the added State-local tax revenues will be used either to retire existing debt or to reduce current borrowing rather than to increase expenditures. Whether the net result will be expansionary will depend upon whether the proportion of additional tax revenues spent on goods and services by State and local government units is greater or smaller than the proportion which would have been spent by the taxpayers from whom they collect the additional taxes. But whether or not the response of State and local government units is such as to strengthen the aggregate impact of Federal tax reduction on income and employment, the Federal tax program will ease, to some extent, the problems of these units in obtaining revenues needed to finance urgent public activities, such as education, transportation facilities, and urban development.

SUMMARY OF EFFECTS ON GNP

Tax reductions for consumers will have initial direct effects on the demand for goods and services, as consumers raise their spending level to reflect their higher after-tax incomes. Corporate tax reductions and the lower tax rates applicable to the highest personal income brackets will stimulate investment directly, through raising the rate of return on new investments and providing additional funds for their financing.

These direct or initial effects on spending would occur even if total output, employment, and incomes remained unchanged. But the increased spending cannot fail to increase total output, employment, and incomes. And as activity responds to the initially increased level of spending, cumulative impacts begin to develop in which the several elements interact to carry the expansion far beyond its initial point.

The higher incomes which consumers receive from the added production of both consumer and capital goods will lead to a further step-up in the rate of spending, creating further increases in incomes and spending. The same expansion process raises rates of capacity utilization, thereby interacting with the initial impact of tax reduction on business incomes to make investment both for modernization and expansion more profitable. This in turn generates higher consumer incomes and more spending, helping to provide the added demand which justifies the higher investment.

If there were no investment stimulus—either initially, or as a result of the cumulative process of expansion—we could expect that GNP would ultimately expand by about $16 billion. If the result were no more than this, the tax reduction would still be abundantly rewarding in terms of greater production, employment, purchasing power, and profits. What will really be given up to produce added output will be only unwanted idleness of workers (whose families have reduced neither their needs nor aspirations) and incomplete utilization of plant and machinery (which have continued to depreciate).

But the pay-off is much more than this purely consumption impact. There is also an investment impact, and each extra dollar of investment that is stimulated should bring roughly another dollar of added consumption and encourage still further investment.

Weak Links in the Multiplier Chain

MILTON FRIEDMAN

Milton Friedman is Paul S. Russell Distinguished Service Professor of Economics at the University of Chicago. Friedman's criticisms of multiplier analysis appeared in his book, Capitalism and Freedom (1962).

I SHOULD LIKE to discuss the view, now so widely held, that an increase in governmental expenditures relative to tax-receipts is necessarily expansionary and a decrease contractionary. This view, which is at the heart of the belief that fiscal policy can serve as a balance wheel, is by now almost taken for granted by businessmen, professional economists, and laymen alike. Yet it cannot be demonstrated to be true by logical considerations alone, has never been documented by empirical evidence, and is in fact inconsistent with the relevant empirical evidence of which I know.

The belief has its origin in a crude Keynesian analysis. Suppose governmental expenditures are raised by $100 and taxes are kept unchanged. Then, goes the simple analysis, on the first round, the people who received the extra hundred dollars will have that much more income. They will save some of it, say one-third, and spend the remaining two-thirds. But this means that on the second round, someone else receives an extra $66⅔ of income. He in turn will save some and spend some, and so on and on in infinite sequence. If at every stage one-third is saved and two-thirds spent, then the extra $100 of government expenditures will ultimately, on this analysis, add $300 to income. This is the simple Keynesian multiplier analysis with a multiplier of three. Of course, if there is one injection, the effects will die off, the initial jump in income of $100 being succeeded by a gradual decline back to the earlier level. But if government expenditures are kept $100 higher per unit of time, say $100 a year higher, then, on this analysis, income will remain higher by $300 a year.

This simple analysis is extremely appealing. But the appeal

is spurious and arises from neglecting other relevant effects of the change in question. When these are taken into account, the final result is much more dubious: it may be anything from no change in income at all, in which case private expenditures will go down by the $100 by which government expenditures go up, to the full increase specified. And even if money income increases, prices may rise, so real income will increase less or not at all. Let us examine some of the possible slips 'twixt cup and lip.

In the first place, nothing is said in the simple account about what the government spends the $100 on. Suppose, for example, it spends it on something that individuals were otherwise obtaining for themselves. They were, for example, spending $100 on paying fees to a park which paid the cost of attendants to keep it clean. Suppose the government now pays these costs and permits people to enter the park "free." The attendants still receive the same income, but the people who paid the fees have $100 available. The government spending does not, even in the initial stage, add $100 to anyone's income. What it does is to leave some people with $100 available to use for purposes other than the park, and presumably purposes they value less highly. They can be expected to spend less out of their total income for consumer goods than formerly, since they are receiving the park services free. How much less, it is not easy to say. Even if we accept, as in the simple analysis, that people save one-third of additional income, it does not follow that when they get one set of consumer goods "free," two-thirds of the released money will be spent on other consumer goods. One extreme possibility, of course, is that they will continue to buy the same collection of other consumer goods as they did before and add the released $100 to their savings. In this case even in the simple Keynesian analysis, the effect of the government expenditures is completely offset: government expenditures go up by $100, private down by $100. Or, to take another example, the $100 may be spent to build a road that a private enterprise would otherwise have built or the availability of which may make repairs to the company's trucks unnecessary. The firm then has funds released, but presumably will not spend them all on what are less attractive investments. In these cases, government expenditures simply divert private expenditures and only the net excess of government expenditures is even available at the outset for the multiplier to work on. From this point of view, it is paradoxical that the way to assure no diversion is to have the government spend the money for something utterly useless—this is the limited intellectual content to the "filling-holes" type of make-work. But of course this itself shows that there is something wrong with the analysis.

In the second place, nothing is said in the simple account about where the government gets the $100 to spend. So far as the analysis goes, the results are the same whether the government prints extra money or borrows it from the public. But surely which it does will make a difference. To separate fiscal from monetary policy, let us suppose the government borrows the $100 so that the stock of money is the same as it would have been in the absence of the government expenditure. This is the proper assumption because the stock of money can be increased without extra government expenditure, if that is desired, simply by printing the money and buying outstanding government bonds with it. But we must now ask what the effect of borrowing is. To analyze this problem, let us assume that diversion does not occur, so in the first instance there is no direct offset to the $100 in the form of a compensating drop in private expenditures. Note that the government's borrowing to spend does not alter the amount of money in private hands. The government borrows $100 with its right hand from some individuals and hands the money with its left hand to those individuals to whom its expenditures go. Different people hold the money but the total amount of money held is unchanged.

The simple Keynesian analysis implicitly assumes that borrowing the money does not have any effects on other spending. There are two extreme circumstances under which this can occur. First, suppose people are utterly indifferent to whether they hold bonds or money, so that bonds to get the $100 can be sold without having to offer a higher return to the buyer than such bonds were yielding before. (Of course, $100 is so small an amount that it would in practice have a negligible effect on the required rate of return, but the issue is one of principle whose practical effect can be seen by letting the $100 stand for $100 million or $100 ten-million.) In Keynesian jargon, there is a "liquidity trap" so people buy the bonds with "idle money." If this is not the case, and clearly it cannot be indefinitely, then the government can sell the bonds only by offering a higher rate of return on it. A higher rate will then have to be paid also by other borrowers. This higher rate will in general discourage private spending on the part of would-be borrowers. Here comes the second extreme circumstance under which the simple Keynesian analysis will hold: if potential borrowers are so stubborn about spending that no rise in interest rates, however steep, will cut down their expenditures, or, in Keynesian jargon, if the marginal efficiency schedule of investment is perfectly inelastic with respect to the interest rate.

I know of no established economist, no matter how much of a Keynesian he may regard himself as being, who would regard either of these extreme assumptions as holding currently, or as being capable of holding over any considerable range of borrowing or rise in interest rates, or as having held except under rather special circumstances in the past. Yet many an economist, let alone non-economist, whether regarding himself as Keynesian or not, accepts as valid the belief that a rise in governmental expenditures relative to tax receipts, even when financed by borrowing, is *necessarily* expansionist, though as we have seen, this belief implicitly requires one of these extreme circumstances to hold.

If neither assumption holds, the rise in government expenditures will be offset by a decline in private expenditures on the part either of those who lend funds to the government, or of those who would otherwise have borrowed the funds. How much of the rise in expenditures will be offset? This depends on the holders of money. The extreme assumption, implicit in a rigid quantity theory of money, is that the amount of money people want to hold depends, on the average, only on their income and not on the rate of return that they can get on bonds and similar securities. In this case, since the total stock of money is the same before and after, the total money income will also have to be the same in order to make people just satisfied to hold that money stock. This means that interest rates will have to rise enough to choke off an amount of private spending exactly equal to the increased public expenditure. In this extreme case, there is no sense at all in which the government expenditures are expansionary. Not even money income goes up, let alone real income. All that happens is that government expenditures go up and private expenditures down.

I warn the reader that this is a highly simplified analysis. A full analysis would require a lengthy textbook. But even this simplified analysis is enough to demonstrate that any result is possible between a $300 rise in income and a zero rise. The more stubborn consumers are with respect to how much they will spend on consumption out of a given income, and the more stubborn purchasers of capital goods are with respect to how much they will spend on such goods regardless of cost, the nearer the result will be to the Keynesian extreme of a $300 rise. On the other side, the more stubborn money holders are with respect to the ratio they wish to maintain between their cash balances and their income, the closer the result will be to the rigid quantity theory extreme of no change in income. In which of these respects the public is more stubborn is an empirical question to be judged from the factual evidence, not something that can be determined by reason alone.

Before the Great Depression of the 1930s, the bulk of economists would unquestionably have concluded that the result would be nearer to no rise in income than to a $300 rise. Since then, the bulk of economists would unquestionably conclude the opposite. More recently, there has been a movement back toward the earlier position. Sad to say, none of these shifts can be said to be based on satisfactory evidence. They have been based rather on intuitive judgments from crude experience.

In co-operation with some of my students, I have done some fairly extensive empirical work, for the United States and other countries, to get some more satisfactory evidence.[1] The results are striking. They strongly suggest that the actual outcome will be closer to the quantity theory extreme than to the Keynesian. The judgment that seems justified on the basis of this evidence is that the assumed $100 increase in government expenditures can on the average be expected to add just about $100 to income, sometimes less, sometimes more. This means that a rise in government expenditures relative to income is not expan-

1. Some of the results are contained in Milton Friedman and David Meiselman, "The Relative Stability of the Investment Multiplier and Monetary Velocity in the United States, 1896–1958," in *Stabilization Policies* (Commission on Money and Credit, 1963).

sionary in any relevant sense. It may add to money income but all of this addition is absorbed by government expenditures. Private expenditures are unchanged. Since prices are likely to rise in the process, or fall less than they otherwise would, the effect is to leave private expenditures smaller in real terms. Converse propositions hold for a decline in government expenditures.

These conclusions cannot of course be regarded as final. They are based on the broadest and most comprehensive body of evidence I know about, but that body of evidence still leaves much to be desired.

One thing is however clear. Whether the views so widely accepted about the effects of fiscal policy be right or wrong, they are contradicted by at least one extensive body of evidence. I know of no coherent or organized body of evidence justifying them. They are part of economic mythology, not the demonstrated conclusions of economic analysis or quantitative studies. Yet they have wielded immense influence in securing widespread public backing for far-reaching governmental interference in economic life.

Functional Fiscal Policy for the 1960s

PAUL A. SAMUELSON

In the Wicksell Lectures, delivered in Sweden in 1961, Professor Samuelson covered a wide range of topics relating to "Stability and Growth in the American Economy." In this selection he comments on American fiscal policy.

DEFICIT FOLKLORE VS. ECONOMICS

THE REAL BARRIER to optimal fiscal policy is not procedural or administrative. It is ideological. If the American people, Congress, and the President all had a desire for the requisite pattern of expenditure and taxing—and the implied budget deficits (and surpluses!)—then without any structural reforms our present system could be more nearly optimally stabilizing. It is simply a matter of fact, though, that Americans attach great ideological importance to that particular arbitrary magnitude which is called the administrative budget. The American public simply cannot stomach budgetary deficits of the size sometimes needed for stability, high employment and growth. Or, what is really an indistinguishable variant, the American public cannot be persuaded or persuade itself that such sizable deficits are truly needed and feasible.

Foreigners may find this surprising. Economists may find it shocking. They may point out that a year is an arbitrary unit and that since the budget cannot be balanced in every day or every month, there is no particular merit in trying to balance it in the arbitrary astronomical cycle involved in one swing of the earth around the sun. Why not balance it over some other cycle, say the business cycle? Or over the nineteen year cycle of Easter? Or over a decade?

And why balance the so-called administrative budget? It differs from, and is inferior to, the cash budget, which nets out purely bookkeeping items that involve no flow of funds between government and the public. But why jettison one shibboleth only to take on another? The cash budget itself is inferior as a measure of the government's current impact on the economy to the budget on national income account, which takes into consideration the accruals of corporate tax liability as they occur and become a crucial factor in corporate spending decisions. While the administrative budget is probably the least meaningful and useful of these three budget concepts, none of them takes into account public capital formation and the increase in assets that is taking place in the governmental sector. It has long been argued that America should adopt some form of a capital budget which will distinguish between current and capital items and will bring to attention the public assets that offset the public debt.

An informed economist knows that no single concept of the budget can do justice to the qualitative and quantitative aspects of fiscal policy. No single one can be set up in advance as the desirable goal to be "balanced" in any year, month, business cycle, or decade. Changing the focus of attention from one concept to another one may minimize the economic harm resulting from ideological attitudes. Or changing from focussing upon one concept to spreading attention over several may serve to blunt and confuse ideological preoccupations. In principle, though, there is only one correct rule about budget balance—Smith's Law (not from Adam Smith but Professor Warren Smith of the University of Michigan). It goes as follows:

Smith's Law. There is only one rule about budget balancing, and it is that the budget should never be balanced.

Never? Well, hardly ever. Economic conditions will generally call for either a surplus or a deficit. Only in the transition as the budget is passing from the black to the red (or from the red to the black) should the budget be fleetingly in balance.

Avoiding Inflation or Deflation · My nine-year-old boy asked me recently "Why should there be taxes? Why not just print money to pay for the goods government needs?" He is a dangerous character. The next thing I know he will be questioning capital punishment, the law of gravity, and my own infallibility. But in nine more years he will have learned the facts of life and come to regard his question as a foolish one. Imagine questioning the inevitability of taxes, or death!

It will take another nine years of advanced study in economics before he comes to appreciate the wisdom of his question and the proper answer to it. As given by A. P. Lerner, that answer would go roughly as follows.

Never tax just for the sake of taxing. Tax primarily to reduce the pressure of excessive dollar demand for society's current limited resources, which are limited because of their scarcity in relationship to government and private bids for them. If the sum of private and public dollar demand is sufficiently great, you should legislate taxes great enough to produce a large and persistent budget surplus. If the total of dollar demand is chronically low relative to the value of total resources available at current prices, economic prudence requires you to legislate tax rates low enough to result in a budget deficit. Such a deficit, which results from the indicated pattern of public expenditure and taxes, can be counted on to produce expansionary stimulus needed to offset the deflationary pressures in the economic system. This government stimulus is not more expansionary nor more inflationary than would be an equivalent billions of dollar increase in spontaneous family expenditure on consumption or spontaneous pickup in investment spending.

Budget balance is itself irrelevant. Such a point of balance could be much too inflationary at certain times and deflationary at others. The effects of a budget balance with public expenditure and taxes both high cannot be expected to be the same as an equivalent balance achieved when low taxes match low expenditures. While a nine-year-old might be forgiven for not realizing it, we should know that financing substantial public expenditures by the printing of new money would probably be swelling the total value of dollar spending beyond the likely surplus of private saving over private investment. So we tax just enough to avoid such an inflationary gap, financing the algebraic difference by nothing so crude as the printing of Treasury currency, instead relying upon optimal debt management and central banking credit creation.

I had a teacher who was seven times nine years old but the doctrine of *de mortuis nihil nisi bonum* forbids me to reveal his name, which is just as well since he was always something of an unknown soldier. He used to say pithily: "A dollar of expenditure is a dollar of taxes." A glance at public accounts will show there to be billions of exceptions to that theorem. His doctrine is wrong today; and it was obsolete before it had been enunciated, which is something of a *tour de force*. The history of capitalism, and perhaps of the Darwinian ascent of man, is a history of deficits outweighing surpluses. This is not a matter of mankind living beyond its means but rather up to them. . . .

NARROWING THE GAP

We are not now living up to our potential. So America could achieve very rapid short-term growth just by getting unemployment down from 5½ percent to 4 percent, and excess capacity down from say 20 percent to 10 percent.

Popular discussion, particularly in liberal circles, has quite naturally put the greatest emphasis on achieving rapid (near-term) growth through restoring full employment. To move nearer to full employment, an increase in consumption, investment, or government spending is needed.

Expanding Government Expenditures · So liberals often propose that more be spent on urban renewal, conservation, health and other programs, both because such programs are desired for their own sake and also because (like digging ditches and filling them up again) such government expenditure programs result in increased money and real income, with multiplier effects on consumption and perhaps investment spending, and regardless of whether such programs have any direct bearing on our growth potential.

Expanding Consumption · The same people urge that tax rates be reduced so that consumption spending, particularly of the lower-income ready-spenders, be increased. Such consumption itself adds to the increase in GNP, and in addition can be expected to have secondary effects of a multiplier kind on further consumption and perhaps investment. . . .

Expanding Investment · Fiscal policy could also be directed toward direct stimulus to investment. President Kennedy early proposed an *investment tax credit* to induce greater net capital formation. This concession to business met a cold reception from businessmen for reasons that lie outside economics: after a long legislative struggle, such an investment tax credit was passed, involving reduced rates and no longer involving extra credit for firms which expanded their investments from earlier levels.

More *rapid depreciation,* which had made some headway in Eisenhower's 1954 tax act, was scheduled to go into effect in 1962. Such measures, to the degree that they permit depreciation more rapid than actual decline in economic value as a result of obsolescence and physical wear, represent an interest-free loan to business with the favorable feature that the loan has to be paid back only if business subsequently has taxable income. Like the investment credit, it should provide some extra funds available for investment and increase the incentive to use other funds for investment. Since I am adding quiet remarks, I ought to say softly that the competitive race between the various developed countries of the world to give the fastest depreciation rates has gone beyond the point where true economic depreciation is recognized by the tax authorities; it is now at the point where loopholes have been deliberately created in tax systems alleging to tax (money and not real) earnings, with the design of giving a bribe and bait to expand investment and employment. It is like the case of our municipalities, which vie with each other to give greater tax concessions in order to lure firms away from other areas.

In America we have a double layer of income taxation. Ford Motors is taxed in its earning at a marginal rate of 52 percent, regardless of how much it pays out in dividends; then whatever is paid out in dividends is taxed to the person who receives the dividends at essentially his regular marginal rate of personal income tax. A *reduction in the corporate tax rate* to below 52 percent might be expected to have some favorable effect upon capital formation. Thus, if managers insist on a 10 percent yield after taxes before they will build a plant and if the pre-tax yield is now only 20 percent, they will not build that plant. However, if the corporate tax rate were cut from 52 percent down to below 50 percent, that investment project would now become worthwhile. Moreover, as firms accumulate more money because of the rate reduction, they may bid down the postulated 10 percent after-tax yield needed to induce certain kinds of risky investment.

Liberals argue that it is inequitable to help owners of property too much. They also argue that, with investment so sluggish in the American economy of recent years, there will be an inelastic stimulus to investment from such tax reductions. On the other hand, more conservative people argue that since it is investment that has been so disappointing in recent years, tax reduction should be specially directed toward it—either as a matter of equity, or because its marginal social worth is so great, or because of a presumed elasticity of its response.

Leaving ethical judgments to the side, my observation of the behavior of decision makers and of their cash positions and opportunities suggests to me that in the short run there is not a great deal of potency in corporation tax reduction. In the longer run, combined with a vigorous full-employment problem and taking into account the international balance constraint on credit ease, there may be merits in such programs in accelerating the "deepening of capital" so helpful for a growth program.

PUBLIC THRIFT

For half a dozen years I have been preaching the doctrine that a mixed-enterprise economy can raise its rate of capital formation, and hence the growth rate of potential GNP, by supplementing private thrift by public thrift. Just as people decide their day-to-day decisions about consuming and nonconsuming in the marketplace for goods, for bonds and saving accounts and for equities, so they may voluntarily come together at the political polls and vote for an additional rate of capital formation to be brought about through government action. I do not have in mind here merely that people may vote for durable dams, school buildings, and other forms of social capital, even though such programs may well be desirable for their own sakes and for growth. What I mean is that we may all democratically vote that our full-employment mix of output should be shifted toward more capital formation and less consumption by a package of the following devices:

1. *Expansionary monetary policies* by the central bank and other credit agencies is to make credit more available and cheaper to potential investors. With effective interest rates low, investment projects which previously didn't pay unless they yielded (say) a 10 percent equity yield, now will be profitable to carry through. Then 9 percent projects can be made to be profit-

able by further credit-expansion programs, thereby causing the stimulus to growth coming from technical change to be supplemented by greater "induced capital deepening" than would otherwise have been the case.

2. *Austere fiscal policies* will also be necessary whenever Step 1's monetary ease induces so much private investment as to open up an inflationary gap of excessive dollar spending. By raising or maintaining tax rates enough relative to needed government expenditure on current and capital goods and on welfare transfers, we can lower the share of total income accruing to private persons and firms, thereby causing the reduction in consumption needed to release the scarce resources in our postulated full-employment economy that are needed for the induced investment programs. The two-step program for growth has not even been tested yet because it was never able to get off the ground: Step 1, involving militant monetary expansion, has never taken place because our international deficit would not permit us to have really low short-term and long-term interest rates. Hence, we have no real evidence as to the potency or impotence of easy money to induce capital formation of a deepening kind.

While the factual issue is still open, from the viewpoint of policy in the early 1960s the verdict is clear. So long as we cannot introduce Step 1 of the new-look program, Step 2 is clearly undesirable and the whole program must be for some time soft-pedaled. It would be too dramatic to say that we are in an era of stagnation. Perhaps it will sound better if we say that we *may* be in one of the slack periods of the so-called Kuznets long waves, which at 15- to 25-year intervals seem to appear in American annals of the last 75 years (in construction data, population and immigration data, in various measures involving the scale of economic resources *and their degree of intensity* of utilization).

We no longer regard such swings as immutable facts of nature, like the inevitable plagues that man could do nothing about before the age of penicillin, sulpha, medical care, and public health. Fiscal and monetary policies can ameliorate, moderate, and perhaps even compensate fully for such tendencies toward sluggish investment opportunities. But until we regain freedom of domestic monetary policy or experiment further with unconventional credit policies—such as helpful guarantees that reduce riskiness of domestic investment without sending funds abroad to get higher yields in London and other money markets —we must welcome anything which increases public or private consumption.

CONCLUSION

Ours, for the most part, are the happy problems that come with affluence. We have made strides toward solving many of them, and shall be making further strides these next few years. But we do not make progress by being complacent or by sticking to ancient orthodoxies. That reasoning suggested long ago and events of the last few years have amply confirmed.

Moreover, we still have one non-economic obstacle to overcome. I refer to Americans' ideological repugnance for continuing budgetary deficits. It must be evident to any attentive listener that my diagnosis of recent economic history has the implication that the United States *may* be in prudent need of sizable deficits in the administrative budget for at least the next few years of the 1960s and perhaps even longer. As the lungs need air, the heart needs blood and the stomach needs food—and not as a drunkard needs drink, an addict needs dope, and a diabetic needs insulin—a modern economy may in some epochs need chronic deficits and a growing public debt (and in other epochs need a chronic surplus, i.e., a chronic overtaxation to release resources to investment needs and to curtail inflation and to reduce the public debt). I say this in all seriousness even though scarcely one in a hundred of our opinion makers can yet comprehend my meaning. But here too I am optimistic that rationality will win out over habit.

The Need for Balanced Federal Budgets

MAURICE H. STANS

Maurice H. Stans, a distinguished accountant and administrator, was President Eisenhower's Director of the Budget when he presented this paper to the American Academy of Political and Social Science in 1959.

THE FEDERAL government should have a balanced budget; its expenditures, especially in times like these, should not exceed its income. Of this I am deeply convinced.

As a matter of fact, I find it difficult to understand why there are still some people who do not seem to agree. Even though I have now been an official of the government almost four years and know by hard experience that there are at least two sides to all public questions, on this one the facts speak eloquently for themselves. And the arguments that are marshalled in opposition to show that a balanced budget is unimportant—or that it can be safely forsaken for lengthy periods of time—certainly seem unsound. It is true that we as a nation have been extremely fortunate in maintaining our fundamental strengths thus far despite the heavy deficit spending of the past thirty years. But we cannot count on being lucky forever, and more and more the consequences of past profligacy are now catching up with us.

Let us look at some of the facts:

1. It is a fact that in 24 of the last 30 years the federal government has spent more than it has received.

2. It is a fact that last fiscal year the federal government had a deficit (12.5 billion dollars) larger than ever before in time of peace.

3. It is a fact that the federal government debt is now 290 billion dollars and that the annual cost of carrying that debt is more than 10 percent of the budget income of the government—and has been going up.

4. It is a fact that our economy is operating at a higher rate of activity than it ever has before and that the standard of

living it is producing for all America is far beyond that of any other country in the world.

5. It is a fact that in times of high economic activity there is competition among business, consumers, and government for the productive resources of the country; if government, by indulging in high levels of spending in such times, intensifies that competition, it openly invites inflation.

6. It is a fact that with an unbalanced budget, federal borrowings to raise the money to spend more than income tend to add to the money supply of the country and therefore are inflationary.

7. It is a fact that the purchasing power of the dollar has declined more than 50 percent in the last twenty years. Today we spend more than $2.00 to get what $1.00 would buy in 1939.

8. And finally, it is a fact that all too often in history inflation has been the undoing of nations, great and small.

In my view, the facts that I have recited clearly demonstrate the need for:

1. Containing federal expenditures within federal income— which means balancing the budget.

2. Establishing the principle of a balanced budget—including some surplus for reduction of the national debt—as a fiscal objective for the prosperous years ahead.

These are the standards on which fiscal integrity for the nation should rest. These are the standards by which the force of inflation induced by reckless fiscal policy can be averted. Yet in 24 of the last 30 years we have not been able to attain them.

Let us look at some of the circumstances which have caused heavy federal spending in the past and have, perhaps, made us insensitive to the dangers of deficits.

LOOKING BACK

Over the last three decades the federal government has spent 264 billion dollars more than it has received. The six years in which there was an excess of income over expense produced negligible surpluses in relation to the deficits of the other years.

We need hardly be reminded of the cause of most of those deficits. In the earlier years it was depression; in the middle years it was war; in recent years it has been war again and then recession.

In the depression years it was not possible to balance the budget; while government services and costs were growing by popular demand, federal revenues declined as a result of economic inactivity. The efforts made to balance the budget by increasing tax rates in 1930 and 1932 and in 1936 to 1938 were apparently self-defeating.

As for the expenditure side of the budget, the decade of the 1930s produced a great deal of talk about "pump-priming" and "compensatory spending"—federal spending which would compensate in poor times for the decline in business and consumer demand and thus lend balance and stability to the economy. The theory was, of course, for the federal government to spend proportionately larger amounts during depression times and proportionately smaller amounts during good times—to suffer deficits in poor years and enjoy surpluses in prosperous years, with the objective of coming out even over the long pull.

Then, in the early 1940s came World War II. During the war years, the federal government's expenditures vastly exceeded its income, and huge further deficits were piled up. In retrospect, most students of wartime economic developments now agree that we did not tax ourselves nearly enough. We did not pay enough of the costs of war out of current income. We created a large debt while suppressing some of its inflationary consequences with direct economic controls, but the suppression was only temporary.

Depression and war, although major factors, were not the only reasons for increased federal expenditures and deficits during the past thirty years. It was more complex than that. In the 1930s the national philosophy of the responsibilities of the federal government underwent a major change. The country's needs for economic growth and social advancement were gradually given increased recognition at the federal level.

The aim of economic growth, of social advancement, and of "compensatory" economic stability became intertwined. Many federal activities of far-reaching implications were established in ways which affected federal expenditures for very long periods of time—if not permanently. Social security, greatly increased support for agriculture, rural electrification, aids to homeowners and mortgage institutions, public housing, public power developments like the Tennessee Valley Authority and other multi-purpose water resource projects, and public assistance grants are just a few examples. All of them, however, remained as federal programs after World War II. And we were actually fighting in that war before federal spending for work relief could be stopped.

The immediate postwar period was marked by dramatic demobilization. Nevertheless, many of the major costs of war lingered on. The maintenance in the postwar period of even the reduced and relatively modest structure of our Armed Forces was far more costly than anything that existed in the way of the machinery of war prior to 1940. The war also left us with greatly increased expenditure commitments for interest on the public debt, for veterans, and for atomic energy. The Marshall Plan and the mutual security program followed in succession. It became obvious, next, that the cold war was going to be expensive. Then, with the Korean aggression, it became necessary to rearm and, even after the shooting stopped, the peacetime striking force and defensive machinery we had to maintain continued expenditures at levels that far exceeded in cost anything we had earlier imagined.

Thus, the postwar growth of the budget has been partly in the area of national security, partly deferred costs of World War II, and partly the inheritance of activities and ways of thinking that characterized the depression of the 1930s. We have now learned that many of the programs the federal government initiated in the 1930s were neither temporary nor "compensatory" in character. Moreover, we have not only retained many of them, but we have also greatly expanded them in the postwar period. Since World War II we have seen large increases in federal expenditures for urban renewal, public health, federal aid for airports and highways, new categories and a higher federal share of public assistance grants, aid to schools in federally impacted areas, great liberalization in aid to agriculture, as well as new programs for science, education, and outer space.

THE PRESENT

What can we conclude from all of this?

It seems to me that in the first place we must recognize that the compensatory theory of federal spending has failed thus far and offers little hope for the future unless we exert a more forceful and courageous determination to control the growth of federal spending. The major spending programs which originated in the depression years have in most cases persisted in the following decades. A work relief project could be turned off when we started to fight a war, but most of the programs established in the 1930s developed characteristics of a far more permanent sort.

An example can be found in the program of the Rural Electrification Administration (REA). This program was started in 1936 when only a minority of farm families enjoyed the benefits of electricity. Today, 95 percent of our farms receive central station electric service. We have invested 4 billion dollars in this program, at 2 percent interest. Nonetheless, indications are that future demands for federal funds will be even greater as the REA co-operatives continue to grow.

The startling fact is that three out of four new users currently being added are nonfarm users. About one-half of REA electric power goes to industries, communities, or nonfarm families. The reasonable approach is that rural electric co-operatives should now be able to get some of their financing from other than government sources, especially for nonfarm purposes that compete with taxed private industry. . . .

Inability to turn off expenditures is not all that is wrong with the compensatory theory of the prewar period. Initially, it dealt largely with the spending side of the fiscal equation whereas the income side now appears to be playing a more important part. Today—with corporate income tax rates at 52 percent—any substantial reduction of corporate earnings produces an immediate proportionate and large loss to the federal treasury. Personal income taxes also respond, though less sharply, to a fall in national production and employment. Thus, when times take a turn for the worse, federal revenues decline promptly and substantially.

Couple this with enlarged social obligations in times of recession or depression—unemployment compensation, public assistance, and so on—and you have substantial leverage of a more or less automatic character for the production of federal deficits in times of depressed economic activity. To do more than this—

to deliberately step up expenditures still more, for public works and other construction, as was done last year—runs grave risks. There is, first, the risk that an antirecession expenditure program cannot be turned off after the recession, but instead represents a permanent increase in the public sphere at the expense of the private. Second, it is difficult to start programs quickly, so the major impact may come long after the need for the economic stimulation has passed. Both of these risks mean that antirecession actions can well represent an inflationary danger for the postrecession period. The danger is there even if, as some believe, positive governmental intervention is required to counter recessions. It is more grave, however, if—and I believe this was proved true in 1958–59—the economy is vigorous and resilient enough to come out of a temporary recession and to go on through a revival period to new prosperous peaks without any direct financial federal interference.

I think we may conclude that it is inevitable that our nation will be faced with large budgets in the years ahead. This is particularly true for the defense obligations which our country has assumed, for its international undertakings to provide economic and military assistance to other free nations, and as a result of many programs which have been started over the years —major programs for water resource development, agriculture, veterans' benefits, low-cost housing, airways modernization, and space exploration—all these and many others have taken on a permanent quality which makes it clear that federal budgets will be large budgets in our lifetimes.

There is still another conclusion which springs from this short recitation of the history of the last thirty years. It is that the federal government has assumed more and more responsibility for activities which formerly were regarded as being under the jurisdiction of state and local governments. More and more the federal government has assumed responsibility for public assistance, housing, urban renewal, educational aid to areas with federal installations, and many other programs that are now supported by federal grants-in-aid to the states. All this, of course, contributes to the conclusion that these federal programs are not only large at the present time, but have a built-in durability—a staying power with which we must reckon as a fact of life.

I think these thoughts are well summarized in the words of Mr. Allen Sproul, former president of the New York Federal Reserve Bank, who recently said:

Government, in our day, touches upon the economic life of the community in an almost bewildering variety of ways, but its overall influence comes into focus in the consolidated cash budget and, in a subsidiary way, in the management of the public debt. When we abandoned the idea of taxation for revenue only and admitted, as we must, a more important role of Government in economic affairs, we thought up a tidy little scheme called the compensatory budget. This envisaged a cash budget balanced in times of real prosperity, in deficit in times of economic recession, and in surplus in times of inflationary boom. What we have got is a budget that may throw up a shaky surplus in times of boom, but that will surely show substantial deficits in times of recession. The bias, over time, is toward deficits, with only wobbly contracyclical tendencies.

LOOKING AHEAD

It seems to me that as we move into another decade it will be essential to recognize that unless we have a more positive program for operating our federal government within its income, the forces that have gained such tremendous momentum in the past will perpetuate the tradition of deficits—to the great disadvantage of the country as a whole.

Assuming a continuous, but not uninterrupted, economic growth for the country, accompanied by ever-increasing, but not uninterrupted, growth of federal revenues, we should nevertheless expect that the growth of programs started in the past will have a strong tendency to absorb the expected additional revenues—unless aggressive controls are exercised by an alert administration and a statesmanlike Congress during those years. . . .

The lesson is clear. We should pay as we go, and if we are to look for debt reduction or tax reduction on a sound footing—as we should—we must do more than this. We must plan for substantial budgetary surpluses in good years—or we will surely contribute to further dangerous inflation in the years ahead.

The Limitations of Public Works

WILFRED LEWIS, JR.

Wilfred Lewis, Jr., former staff economist in the Bureau of the Budget, wrote this essay for the November 1961 issue of Challenge. Drawing on both his government experience and his research at The Brookings Institution, he reached rather pessimistic conclusions on the role of public works as a stabilizer.

. . . THE FIRST ORDER of business in fighting any recession is to get people back to work. Since the beginning of the Great Depression the most frequent answer to the problem—advanced by politicians and laymen, as well as professional economists—has been "public works."

The popularity of public works spending as a pump priming device is not hard to understand. It would obviously be inefficient to try to step up many ordinary government activities—say, internal revenue audits, or patent investigations or customs inspections—to offset trends in the level of private employment. But a few years more or less spent in constructing an office building, or a dam or a highway which will have a useful life of 50 to 100 years seems not only harmless but useful.

What use was actually made of public works spending during the four periods of high unemployment since World War II? Could it have been used more effectively?

The first postwar recession began in October, 1948. The Truman Administration's reaction, however, came rather slowly. Not only did the recession go unmentioned in the annual Presidential messages the following January, but the messages diagnosed the economy's principal problem as being inflation. . . .

While there was some concern in business and academic quarters, the official attitude in Washington, once it was realized that inflation had in fact ceased, was that no more than a temporary respite was taking place and a little "disinflation" after the sharp postwar price rises of 1946 and 1948 would do no harm.

The sharp recovery in the first half of 1950 was sparked by renewed private demands for housing and automobiles, and received no stimulus from public works or other deliberate countercyclical actions. By mid-1950, when the Korean war turned attention from lingering unemployment to the renewed threat of inflation, the recovery was substantially completed.

The end of the Korean war in 1953 coincided with the efforts of the newly installed Eisenhower Administration to stretch out defense procurement and cut back nondefense spending. The resulting drop in government orders and expenditures, which continued to decline until well into 1954, was a major factor in the recession which began in the second half of 1953.

On January 1, 1954, individual income tax rates dropped back about 10 percent, as scheduled under the 1951 Korean war revenue act, and the excess profits tax was finally allowed to die. . . .

Aside from the tax cuts, which probably would have taken place anyway, the major discretionary action to fight the [1953–54] recession was an attempt to reschedule fiscal 1955 expenditures as early in the year as possible without affecting the total budget. Although a number of programs were affected by this move—such as defense, lead and zinc stockpiling, and shipbuilding subsidies—the public works totals involved were quite small. Starting in mid-1953 there had been several attempts to coordinate and classify public works so that a "shelf" of useful federal projects would be ready to start on short notice if needed. But these were not used during the recession and, in fact, it is doubtful if the shelf actually existed except in name. Later, in 1954, the Congress enacted a program of loans to localities for the advance planning of public works projects. But, few such loans were made by the middle of 1955, when recovery was substantially complete, and the program was never used for counterrecession purposes.

In the recession of 1957–58 discretionary expenditure increases, including public works, were used more freely than they had been in the two previous postwar downturns. The recession advanced more rapidly and resulted in higher levels of unemployment than either of the others. Recovery after the April, 1958 low point was also more rapid than in 1949 or 1954, giving rise to the description of 1957–58 as the "plunging neckline" recession. Although the January, 1958 Economic Report hinted at continued recession, the budget stressed restraint in expenditures in general and a policy of no new public works starts in particular. The Administration's attitude, once the recession was acknowledged, was that corrective fiscal policy would probably not be required, but if it were, it should be in the nature of tax cuts rather than "make-work" expenditures.

However, a number of steps were taken with and without Congressional action, all on the expenditure side. A temporary 50 percent extension of eligibility periods for unemployment benefits was enacted. The Federal National Mortgage Association was given $1 billion to purchase GI mortgages on new low-cost houses. Civilian agencies of the government were directed to speed procurement of supplies and equipment, and were given blanket authority to purchase up to half of anticipated fiscal 1959 supplies and equipment in advance of specific appropriations. Loan criteria were relaxed in certain federal credit programs. States, localities and private parties were asked to speed action under various programs supported by federal grants or loans.

In the public works field, a general policy of speeding up work on approved civil projects for which funds were available was ordered by the President in March, 1958. Supplemental appropriations for 1959 were requested to enable the speed-up to continue into that year. Congress passed a resolution asking that military construction be similarly accelerated. A Post Office modernization program was announced. Regular highway grants were increased, and a special $400 million authorization was passed for grants to states for additional highway work that could be started quickly.

A program of federal loans for construction of local public works again received strong support in Congress as an anti-recession move; but it failed to pass. A multibillion-dollar river and harbor authorization bill was passed with some claims that it would stimulate employment, but it had no significance as a counterrecession measure because of the long lead-times involved in starting new projects in the water resource field.

Of the various public works actions, the highway program was the most important, although there is no way to tell for sure to what extent the increased federal grants substituted for, rather than added to, state-financed highway outlays that would have taken place anyway. The fact that federal loans were made available for part of the state share of the cost helped keep this "substitution" effect to a minimum, since the states are ordinarily hard put to raise matching funds on short notice. The speed-up of construction of other civilian projects added something over $100 million, perhaps as much as $200 million, to federal outlays during the recovery stage. There is no evidence in end-of-year budget figures that a speed-up in military construction in fact took place. The Post Office modernization program got started about in time for the next recession; only minor amounts of contracts had been let by June, 1960.

There is little doubt that the discretionary actions helped recovery, but public works were only part of the story. Temporary extended unemployment compensation was probably as important as the various public works actions combined. . . .

As before, counterrecession actions were confined to the expenditure side of the budget [in the 1960–61 recession]. The Kennedy Administration made no secret of its belief that both defense and nondefense federal spending had been unduly restricted before it took office. Moreover, since the size of the gap promised a long period before full employment would be approached, it was argued that slow-starting programs with long lead-times could safely be initiated without fear that their later expenditures would come at a time of inflationary pressures. Thus, in the spurt of activity that started in February, 1961, proposals to counter the recession as soon as possible by means of expenditure increases were made at the same time as proposals to expand programs for longer range goals.

Temporary extended unemployment compensation along the lines of the 1958 program, aid to children of the unemployed, extra GI insurance dividends and a general speed-up of procurement and construction under existing programs—these were primarily antirecession in nature. Not primarily related to the recession were proposals for stepped-up authorizations for health and welfare programs, urban renewal, defense, space, college housing, public facility loans, aid to education and medical care for the aged. Other proposals, reflecting a mixture of antirecession and long-range goals, were liberalization of social security benefits to be offset later by higher payroll tax rates, increased farm price supports, an expansion of the school lunch and surplus food disposal programs, "cost of living" increases in veteran's compensation benefit rates, and new programs for retraining and relocating the unemployed, and for grants and loans to depressed areas.

Rising defense and other federal outlays were a big factor in the sharp rise in the economy starting in the second quarter [of 1961]. But the role of public works in the recovery has been minor. As in previous recessions, a major program of federal loans for local public works received strong support in Congress but was not enacted. The Administration catalogued and considered a broad expansion of federal public works involving additional new starts, but has so far relied on speeding up projects already under way or already scheduled for starting. There is little evidence that the speed-up had much effect in the public works field. . . .

In summary, while discretionary antirecession actions helped spur activity during three of the four postwar recoveries, significantly so in two of these, the role of public works, with the possible exception of highways during the 1958–59 recovery, has been modest. Moreover, deliberate counterrecession actions in total have been less important than expenditure increases (or tax cuts) undertaken for other reasons. Whether the government should have taken more vigorous steps to promote recovery has been argued both ways. But for a number of reasons there is evidence that a greater attempt to use public works would not have substantially hastened any of the postwar recoveries.

Planning public works projects of any size requires a considerable period of time. There must be surveys of the land, engineering studies, a calculation of costs and benefits, Congressional authorization of specific projects, postauthorization planning in more specific terms and then Congressional appropriation of necessary funds. Depending on the size and type of project, these steps may require several years.

Not all federal public works, however, are large and inflexible. Flexibility exists for small projects not involving elaborate planning or the acquisition of new land. There is also some flexibility in the form of deferred maintenance and repair, modernization and rehabilitation of existing structures. The total size of such programs, however, is in the tens of millions of dollars, so that a considerable expansion of them would provide only a modest impact on the economy.

Speeding up the rate of work on going projects is a better means of achieving flexibility. Flexibility on going water-resource projects is to some extent limited by the practice of appropriating funds on a year-to-year basis even for multiyear projects, and also by the fact that, once contracts are let, the rate of progress depends essentially on the contractor's initiative. However, if going programs are being held down for budgetary reasons, if there are appropriated funds held in reserve, or if approved and funded new starts are being delayed to minimize the first-year cost, flexibility can be achieved by removing restraints, releasing reserves or moving up the scheduled starting dates.

State-local public works aided by federal grants face similar obstacles, and a few more besides. States or localities have to raise matching funds for grant programs—which may be difficult in recession years. Projects have to be reviewed not only by local authorities but also by the administering federal agency. And it may be difficult to prevent federal grants in the short run from simply replacing rather than adding to construction that would be undertaken with state or local funds anyway.

For these and similar reasons, public works provide only slight potential for releasing spending power on short notice. That potential could be increased if a shelf of fully planned projects were made ready, with money already earmarked, so that they could be started quickly.

There are, on paper, two major shelves of planned projects, but it is easy to exaggerate their importance. In January, 1961, the reserve of authorized federal projects, aside from projects scheduled for starting by the end of fiscal 1962, came to $12 billion, of which $7 billion had plans in process, $4 billion had had no planning and $1 billion was "planned to the stage where contract could be let." By the end of fiscal 1962 an additional $1.5 billion was expected to be fully planned.

However, "planned to stage where contract could be let" does not in fact mean that construction is ready to start. While Congress has granted "authorizations," it has not yet appropriated the money in most cases. Besides that, there is the drawing up of contract specifications, advertising for bids, and then a further wait while bids are opened and a contractor specified. More important, the necessary land has usually not been acquired —this sometimes requires lengthy condemnation proceedings— nor have agreements been worked out with localities on cost sharing. Furthermore, the great bulk of the shelved plans are for large water resource projects—which do not reach peak construction rates for several years.

Under a program initiated in 1954, the Community Facilities Administration has built up a reserve of $3 billion of planned nonfederal projects. However, only a few of these projects qualify for federal assistance during actual construction, and most of the projects have had only the most preliminary planning.

Not only are public works projects slow to start, but, once started, construction may be carried to a stage where it would be difficult or inefficient to try to slow down or stretch out work. This "irreversibility" has probably inhibited more ambitious attempts to use public works in recessions, but its importance has probably been exaggerated. Postwar recessions have been short-lived, but the economy has not always returned to full employment. More important, in an expanding economy in which both public and private outlays may be expected to grow, reversibility need not take the form of an actual decline in construction already begun. It may be sufficient merely to slow the rate at which other new projects are started. This is much easier said than done, but the difficulties are political rather than mechanical.

The successful use of public works to counter recessions requires a shelf of approved, planned projects ready to start, and such a shelf requires either a slowing down once the recession is over, or at least the ability to stop short of actually constructing useful public works that have been fully planned. As a practical matter, planning is generally carried to advanced stages only for projects deemed to have considerable intrinsic merit. For such projects, the fact that the economy happens to be operating at full employment seems to many—certainly to the locality most directly involved and its political spokesmen—an insufficient excuse for delaying construction.

This requirement of a flexible fiscal policy which can work one way during recession and another during full employment rules out several significant categories of public works as potential sources of counterrecession action. Few would argue, for example, that planned, useful missile bases or urban renewal projects ready to start should be delayed because of full employment. Yet, without such restraint, there can hardly be a backlog of projects available for starting in recession periods. . . .

The Formation of Fiscal Policy: 1953–1954

ROBERT J. DONOVAN

Robert J. Donovan, now of the Los Angeles Times, *was a White House correspondent for the New York* Herald-Tribune *during the Eisenhower years. This selection is from his book,* Eisenhower: The Inside Story *(1956).*

PRESIDENT EISENHOWER's immediate reaction to the warning in the Cabinet on September 25, 1953, of an economic decline was that the Republican Party must be ready to use the full power of the government, if necessary, to prevent "another 1929."

The situation described by Arthur F. Burns [1] that morning was one which would have disturbed any administration but which struck a particularly sensitive nerve among members of the party that was just beginning to live down the depression of twenty-five years ago. No one in the White House needed to be reminded that a worse domestic calamity could scarcely befall the United States than a great dislocation of business, finance and farming. This was true not alone because of the personal hardships and political upheaval it would bring but because of the torpedo that economic disaster in America would ram under the free world's defenses against Communism.

By late September it was obvious that the economy was going downhill. The decline was blamed chiefly on excessive inventories, an imbalance of production and sales and the drop in military spending after the truce in Korea.

The administration had taken office during the economic boom of the Korean war. Inflation was then the bugaboo, and in April, 1953, the Secretary of the Treasury moved to tighten credit through the issuance of long-term bonds, which soaked up money that otherwise would have gone into corporate issues or mortgages. This was part of what was popularly called the "hard money" policy. The tightening process was so effective that within a couple of months it brought about, according to the Presi-

1. Then Chairman of the Council of Economic Advisers.—*Editor.*

dent's Economic Report of January, 1954, an "incipient and possibly dangerous scramble" for cash.

The administration soon discovered that the trouble ahead lay in deflation rather than inflation, and the Treasury turned around and, with the Federal Reserve System, took steps to ease credit and make more money available. The fight against deflation was carried a step farther when Humphrey [2] told the convention of the American Bankers Association in Washington on September 22 that the administration would make no effort to prevent the tax changes scheduled for December 31 from taking effect. Indeed, it would have been well nigh politically impossible to have done so. The changes were the expiration of the excess-profits tax and the lapsing of the 10 percent Korea-emergency increase in personal income taxes. Together with the forthcoming reductions in excise taxes, as well as the revisions in the tax law itself, these were expected, when in force a full year, to release $7,400,000,000 in private spending power.

Confronted by signs of deflation, Burns, a pipe-smoking former professor of economics at Columbia University and an authority on the business cycle, told the Cabinet on September 25 that planning was called for as a precaution against further decline.

He said the situation was not critical. The strength of the economy was reflected in such things as its ability to withstand the recent "hard money" credit squeeze, the favorable distribution of income among the people and the basic soundness of the inventory situation.

The Council of Economic Advisers, he added, was thinking less in terms of increased government spending and more in terms of monetary policy, the activities of private business, tax reduction and government programs emphasizing loans rather than construction undertaken by the government itself. Legislation for these purposes, he said, was under study.

Humphrey approved. He pointed out that the credit-easing operations of the Treasury and the Federal Reserve would continue to "release" more money for several months.

The President reminded the Cabinet that in the 1952 campaign the Republicans had promised to use the authority of the government to the maximum to avert a repetition of 1929. The only thing now in question, he stated, was the Republicans' desire to

2. George M. Humphrey, Secretary of the Treasury.—*Editor.*

assure the greatest possible economic activity by the individual.

Humphrey observed that because of recent record-breaking high levels, the only way for the economy to go was down. A few readjustments were not to be feared—employment could decline for six or seven months without becoming critical.

The administration, Eisenhower declared, was sensitive because of the number of "big businessmen" among its officials. He did not believe, he said, that there was any group more concerned about the welfare of the people than this Cabinet. . . .

By November, alarm was widespread not only in the United States but abroad. In the Manchester *Guardian*, an Oxford economist, Dr. Colin Clark, forecast a serious depression in America with unemployment possibly reaching seven million unless the government stepped in with a large spending program. At the turn of the year a persistent clamor for government action was rising from labor and from a number of Democrats, notably Senator Paul H. Douglas, of Illinois, who is an economist.

Week after week, meanwhile, Republican legislative leaders were reporting to Eisenhower that Congress and the country were worried about the recession. With a Congressional election only several months away, the Republican leadership had special cause for worry.

While certain elements of the economy, such as stock prices, had shown signs of improvement, unemployment was rising discouragingly.

The President came under increasingly heavy pressure, especially from labor, to launch a large Federal public works program, and these dismaying statistics added force to it. Walter Reuther demanded action leading toward a "bigger and more prosperous America," and George Meany insisted upon "measures essential to bolster consumer buying and check the present recession before it gains momentum."

Weighing these appeals, Eisenhower spurred plans for an emergency public-works program. But until worst came to worst he continued to ride the squall as his fiscal and economic advisers urged, relying on the economy to right itself with the stimulus of tax reductions, freer credit, liberalized social welfare measures and, above all, confidence by businessmen, home builders, investors and consumers. During this whole period from January through July, 1954, Cabinet meetings and other White House discussions provide a striking picture of a President and his government grappling with trouble in a vast, complicated economy. It is a picture of deep concern but not fright, of urgency but not rashness, of patience but not complacence, of a willingness to act if necessary but a determination not to be stampeded.

Cabinet, January 15, 1954 · Humphrey stated his opinion that prosperity depended more upon the confidence of all the people than upon any particular government measures other than removal of impediments to individual initiative. The President replied that he wished to avoid false expressions of confidence such as were proclaimed in 1929. He wanted to refrain from any suggestion that the government was unable to act positively to strengthen the economy. Dulles agreed that it was necessary to create public confidence by making it clear that the administration knew where it was and where it was going.

Cabinet, February 5, 1954 · The President informed the Cabinet that he had asked Burns to co-ordinate reports from the various departments and agencies on their plans for public-works projects. It would be essential, he said, to have planning advanced sufficiently to insure that men would be put to work quickly Too often, he added, preliminary planning, testing and surveys delay start on work. Projects planned for an emergency program, he insisted, must be intrinsically valuable to national development and must not be merely "made work."

He designated July 1 as a tentative date for the government to be prepared to act.

This was not the end of the matter. Eisenhower said that he was ready then and there to ask Congress for supplemental appropriations for a few immediate projects if any member of the Cabinet recommended it. Projects actually under way, he noted, gave the government flexibility in speeding them up or stretching them out, as conditions required.

McKay [3] spoke up and said that it might be a good idea to initiate several power projects. He mentioned in particular that local government and private interests were prepared to undertake hydro-electric power development at Cougar Dam, a proposed flood-control project on the McKenzie River in Oregon.

3. Douglas McKay, Secretary of the Interior.—*Editor.*

The government, he said, should not lag behind on a "partner-ship" project like this.

The President, who was to place increasing stress on a vast highway construction program, suggested building new toll roads with the government guaranteeing the bonds. Mitchell [4] expressed his eagerness to have something done to check the rise of unemployment in the Pacific Northwest.

Humphrey then made his position known. He said that a broad public-works program would be desirable if operations then in progress should fail to turn the tide. He felt, however, that they might very well succeed.

McKay brought up the point that it was important to get adequate funds to carry through existing projects so that there would be no layoffs of workers.

To cap the discussion Lodge [5] praised the care that was being taken by the administration to master the economic setback. He said that this attitude refuted charges that Republicans were bound to the "trickle down" theory of economics—the theory of helping the few at the top in expectation that the benefits will then seep down to the rest of the people.

(An interesting aspect of this discussion, as well as of similar discussions in the next few months, was the muting of emphasis on balancing the budget. This goal had been emphasized before and was to be emphasized very strongly again. But with the fate of the economy in the balance, it was submerged under the determination of the President and of the Cabinet generally to undertake an expensive public works program if necessary and to prevent a serious depression at any cost.)

Cabinet, March 12, 1954 · The President was in a deadly serious mood. The unemployment situation had worsened. In March the number of jobless reached the peak of 3,725,000, or 5.8 percent of the entire civilian labor force. The fact that unemployment was then at the crest, however, was not known on this date.

Eisenhower said that, of course, the manner of presentation of unemployment statistics had to be discussed. However, he asserted the immediate need was to determine what to do about

4. James Mitchell, Secretary of Labor.—*Editor.*
5. Henry Cabot Lodge, Ambassador to the United Nations.—*Editor.*

unemployment and when to do it. He said that plans had been prepared for countering a decline in the business cycle, but that when one came to look for recommendations as to when these plans should be put into effect, one looked in vain.

Humphrey told the President that Senator Douglas had warned that drastic action should not be taken before unemployment reached the level of 6 or 8 percent of the labor force.

Timely action, the President retorted, would forestall the need for drastic action. Again he insisted at least upon preparedness to act at any moment.

Humphrey, calm as a cucumber, as usual, advised the President against any radical action that could not easily be cut off. Uncertainty as to the fate of the tax-revision bill in Congress, he said, was retarding business, and before any extraordinary action was taken he preferred to wait until April or May to give the picture a chance to clarify. He pointed out that in a period of reduced government expenditures, unemployment was inevitable. As far as he could see, he added, the adverse reaction to the current readjustment was being kept to a minimum.

The President concluded by asking Burns to appear at every subsequent meeting of the Cabinet until further notice to summarize each week's developments and keep all the members alert to the problem.

Cabinet, March 19, 1954 · Burns reported that some favorable trends were appearing, but he urged that judgment be suspended for a while. The Council of Economic Advisers, he said, was moving ahead rapidly with projects that might be started if need should arise.

Stassen [6] suggested that the general confidence of financial circles, evidenced by the steadiness of the stock market, was founded upon a feeling that the administration would take timely action if it was warranted. In his opinion the moment had come for some action, such as increased government purchasing. Burns agreed with his analysis of the reason for confidence in the financial community. Humphrey disagreed. Confidence, he argued, was based on a belief that the government would follow sound fiscal policies and would not act prematurely.

The Democrats were calling for even more spending power

6. Harold Stassen, disarmament adviser.—*Editor.*

in the hands of the people to remedy the recession. A Democratic group, including Senator Walter F. George, of Georgia, had introduced a bill in February to increase the individual income-tax exemptions from $600 to $1,000 in two stages—$200 in 1954 and $200 in 1955. On February 19 Senator Douglas had written the President asking him to back this proposal to head off a possible depression.

The Administration, however, did not withdraw its opposition to the tax bill. At this same meeting of March 19 Humphrey and others remarked that economic trends would play a large part in the fate of the measure (which in amended form was defeated finally).

All the more reason, Eisenhower argued, for the administration to take immediate action to counter the decline and head off the Democrats. Nixon, too, suggested that anything constructive should be done then rather than several months later. Humphrey agreed that projects which the administration would undertake eventually might well be started immediately.

The President urged Burns to have the Council expedite its studies and determine what actions should be taken forthwith.

Cabinet, March 26, 1954 · The sense of mounting urgency continued. Burns had made a list of actions that could be taken, such as modifying Federal Reserve requirements, liberalizing mortgage requirements, altering tax-depreciation policy and hastening domestic procurement. The President asked him to prepare an outline of useful legislation. Humphrey agreed that the administration ought to get additional measures started. Weeks [7] urged faster action on the tanker program, and the President indorsed his suggestion.

Cabinet, April 30, 1954 · Burns came armed with hopeful omens again. Among other things, he noted that, contrary to expectations, the economies of foreign countries had remained strong during the sag in the American economy.

The President told the Cabinet that public works, such as highways, contributed to the future economic strength of the country and should be regarded as investments rather than expenditures.

7. Sinclair Weeks, Secretary of Commerce.—*Editor.*

Cabinet, May 21, 1954 · Rowland R. Hughes, who had recently succeeded Dodge as Budget Director, said that little further reduction was possible in spending on nonsecurity programs. Any substantial cut in the anticipated deficits, he said, would have to come out of security programs. The President then warned sharply against any loose political thinking on budget-balancing. He had refused to promise a balanced budget, he said, by any given date. In toting up its own achievements the administration ought to compare its record with the spending estimates left over by Truman. The Administration was moving in the right direction. It should, he urged, cut out all unnecessary expenditures and thereafter fight for adequate and, if necessary, higher taxes to meet necessary expenses.

Burns suggested that the Democrats might make campaign material out of Truman's fiscal policies on the grounds that the economy had expanded during Truman's administration while the size of the national debt had remained relatively unchanged.

Eisenhower seemed astonished. While some people might wish to make a virtue out of the Democratic record, he replied, the fact remained that the Truman administration had improved the debt situation by a period of virtually complete neglect of national security. Then it undertook a belated preparedness program without any provision for financing it. The result, he added, was first to create a national security crisis and then to pass the bill on to the Eisenhower administration.

Coming up with still more hopeful news, Burns reported that for the third consecutive month the number of increases in orders and production had surpassed the decreases. He said that the economy might be swinging into an upturn.

Cabinet, June 4, 1954 · Again Burns had an optimistic report, this time that the length of the work week had increased slightly in May over April.

The President, however, was still concerned about whether the administration was doing enough. Even though it jarred the logic of some members of the Cabinet, he insisted, everything possible must be done to restore vigor to the economy. It was important, he said, to produce results and to err on the side of doing too much rather than too little. He directed Burns to prepare a complete presentation for the Cabinet on additional actions the administration could take.

Cabinet, June 11, 1954 · Burns made his presentation. He noted definite evidence that recovery was under way, but said the possibility remained that it would fizzle out. He recommended a number of measures, again stressing housing, building, interest rates, and highway construction.

"Arthur, you'd have made a fine chief of staff during the war," the President told him.

Eisenhower said there was a limit to how fast and how far Congress could be pushed. But he ventured the opinion that influential members would recognize the political if not the economic benefits of the housing program if Burns should outline these at a luncheon. . . . The President repeatedly urged that whatever needed to be done should be done quickly, and he asked heads of departments which would be affected by Burns's recommendations to report at the next meeting on what steps might be taken.

This marked the end of the urgency in the Cabinet over the recession. . . .

There was a note of elation in the Cabinet on July 23 when Burns announced that the midyear economic indicators showed definitely that the decline had come to an end. To have passed from the Korean war economy to a peacetime economy without a far more serious drop, he said, was a tremendous accomplishment.

With the Congressional elections approaching, the Cabinet cheerfully discussed various opportunities for making all this clear to the public, especially the now favorable comparison between 1954 and 1952, the last year of Democratic rule.

Toward a Flexible Tax Policy: Automatic and Discretionary Stabilizers

COMMISSION ON MONEY AND CREDIT

The single most sweeping and controversial recommendation of the Commission on Money and Credit called for presidential powers to vary income tax rates, subject to congressional veto. The proposal is spelled out in this discussion of tax policy, taken from the commission's report, Money and Credit *(1961).*

AUTOMATIC STABILIZERS

WITH A GIVEN tax and expenditure structure, changes in total output and income result in automatic changes in tax yields and in certain outlays, the first changing in the same direction as income and the latter in the opposite direction. For example, as personal incomes fall, the yield of the personal income tax falls along with them, while payments for unemployment compensation rise. Consequently, the absolute decline in income available for personal spending is less than the absolute decline in national income. As personal incomes increase, tax yields rise, and unemployment compensation payments decline. These and other similar cushioning effects on fluctuations in the amount of income available to the private sector of the economy occur without legislative or administrative changes in tax and expenditure programs and are thus called *automatic stabilizers.*

The higher the tax rates, the more progressive the rate structure, and the more sensitive the tax base to swings in the cycle, the more will changing tax yields absorb variations in national income, and the smaller will be the remaining change in income available for private spending. The more closely unemployment compensation payments approximate the wage the employee loses, the less will unemployment reduce disposable income. But because tax rates are much less than 100 percent at the margin, and because unemployment compensation is less than the lost wages, changes in national income are only partially offset by the tax and transfer-payment changes. Nevertheless automatic fiscal stabilizers do cushion the fall in income. As a result, private expenditures fall less than they would otherwise. Thus, automatic stabilizers aid recovery by reducing the cumulative deterioration in economic outlook that would otherwise take place and facilitate the forces of recovery contributing to an early upswing. Although the built-in stabilizers are very useful when the economy contracts, they are a mixed blessing when it expands. When business conditions recover from a recession, the federal tax system automatically cuts the growth in private spendable incomes, and hence the expansion tends to proceed more slowly. If the recovery is strong, the automatic stabilizers provide an important and desirable curb to the inflationary pressures that may ensue.

The very size of government expenditures and tax receipts relative to gross national product today, compared with the period before the 1930s, greatly increases the potential cushioning effect of the automatic stabilizers. Whatever the merits or demerits of large government expenditures and tax receipts may be on other grounds, it is clear that the larger they are in relation to the total level of economic activity, the stronger is the impact of the automatic stabilizers. If taxes are equal to 30 percent of GNP, it is apparent that the decline in tax yield with a given fall in GNP will be greater than when taxes account for 10 percent of GNP, and as a consequence the reduction in income available for private expenditures will be less severe. . . .

The effectiveness of the automatic stabilizers does not, however, depend exclusively on the relative size of government expenditures and the level of tax rates. It also depends on the degree to which the tax base (the particular incomes or expenditures subject to tax) fluctuates with changes in the national income and on how tax yields vary with changes in the tax base.

The major portion of federal revenues is derived from the corporation and personal income taxes, both of which (especially the former) are highly sensitive to change in national income. In contrast, local tax receipts, primarily from property taxes, vary little with income. State governments have a wide variety of revenue sources, a large proportion representing general sales taxes or sales and excise taxes levied on particular commodities or services. State tax revenues are therefore much less sensitive to changes in national income than are federal revenues but more so than local revenues.

In addition, state and local governments are less able to borrow than the federal government. Thus, no individual state or local unit of government, acting by itself, has the same capability as the federal government to take countercyclical actions. In addition, since the effects of its fiscal actions are not contained within its own borders but spill over to other areas, they do not have the same incentives.

It follows from the above discussion that the task of maintaining the strength of the automatic stabilizers must be undertaken at the federal level. So long as the major fraction of total government expenditures continues to be made by the federal government, largely because of the size of national security and related outlays, the automatic stabilizers will remain relatively strong. If, however, an improvement in international conditions should permit a substantial reduction in the share of the gross national product required for defense, the power of the automatic stabilizers would be weakened.

In this eventuality the strength of the automatic stabilizers could be partially maintained by modifications which would permit a substitution of the more flexible components of the federal revenue system for the less flexible components of the state and local systems. One means would be to expand the use of federal grants to state and local governments, thereby enabling taxes to be collected at the federal level and spent at the state and local level.

It is impossible to estimate precisely the effectiveness of existing automatic stabilizers. The best available evidence indicates that during the postwar period the built-in flexibility of the federal budget offset between one-third to two-fifths of the fall (or increase) in the gross national product. This is a sizable fraction, far greater than that prevailing before World War II. Recent experience with recurrent and moderately severe recessions raises the question whether the automatic stabilizers can and should be strengthened to play a greater role in reducing the amplitude of cyclical fluctuations. Possible means of increasing the strength of the automatic stabilizers might take the form of greater reliance on more cyclically responsive types of tax revenue and a revision of unemployment insurance.

DISCRETIONARY FISCAL MEASURES

Even if the automatic stabilizers can be improved, discretion-

ary fiscal measures will remain an important instrument of stabilization policy. Consequently, the advantages and disadvan-
tages of possible discretionary actions must be considered. Two
major objections are commonly raised against [them].

The first is that economic forecasts are necessarily so inac-
curate that there is always the possibility that discretionary
action taken on the basis of such forecasts may do more harm
than good. However this objection is applicable to all discretionary stabilization policies, monetary or fiscal. It is a serious
objection, for much is yet to be learned before we can assess the
economic outlook as well as we need to. Nevertheless, the Commission is convinced that judicious use of discretionary measures,
including fiscal policy, cannot be dispensed with.

Secondly, it is frequently alleged that the time required by
Congress to enact discretionary measures and by the executive
to put them into effect may rule them out. For instance, the time
required by Congress to enact tax changes is frequently alleged
to rule out such changes as a desirable means of discretionary
stabilizing action. It is claimed, for example, that the time necessary to enact tax reductions to combat a recession is so long that
they are not likely to take effect until the subsequent recovery
is well underway and that consequently these reductions, enacted
to cut short a recession, may in fact feed a subsequent
boom.

The alleged inability of Congress to act promptly is usually
based on the fact that the passage of major revenue legislation
has been typically an extended process. This was true in the
case of the Revenue Act of 1942, the Revenue Act of 1951, and
the Internal Revenue Code of 1954, all of which took the major
part of a year to enact into final form. These measures, however,
dealt with complicated long-run structural reforms rather than
with short-run problems of economic stabilization. In certain
instances, when emergency conditions dictated a need for speed,
even complicated reforms were put through in a shorter time. For
example, the Revenue Act of 1950 was halted halfway through
its passage as a tax reform measure and sped to enactment as a
substantial tax increase in only 60 days. The Excess Profits
Tax of 1950 was passed within 49 days of a presidential mes-
sage.

Of more relevance as a measure of congressional legislative

speed are the simple tax extension measures, such as those in the postwar period covering the excise and corporate income tax rates. They have generally consumed less than a month's time from the initial action by the Ways and Means Committee. Even the highly controversial extension of the excess profits tax in 1953 required less than 50 days. The temporary extension of unemployment compensation in 1958 was enacted in 73 days, and its extension in 1959 took only 18 days. Debt ceiling increases are the same type of legislation. Prompt hearings and prompt reports could reasonably be expected because of the compelling nature of arresting a boom or stopping a recession.

In sum, when Congress has had straightforward changes before it which it wished to enact, ways have been found to accelerate the legislative process. Fear that action will be delayed by legislative lags, therefore, provides no valid excuse for executive failure to recommend action. These precedents indicate that there is no technical or institutional barrier to a discretionary fiscal policy designed to promote economic stabilization and growth *provided* that the need for such policy is recognized by Congress and the executive and that appropriate discretionary measures are proposed. This conclusion, however, rests on the acceptance of the following basic proposition.

Discretionary fiscal policy requires speed of decision and effect and can only be successful if temporary and reversible fiscal changes for stabilization purposes are dissociated from permanent and structural changes. Techniques should be developed by which taxation and expenditure policies can be applied more flexibly, and the first step in this direction lies in a sharp demarcation between short-run cyclical changes and long-run structural changes. . . .

The tax structure and expenditure programs do change from time to time and must be changed periodically as the growth of the economy alters the tax revenue-expenditure relationship. The periodic reassessment of the relationship between tax revenues and expenditures is necessary. When reassessment indicates the need for changes, it would be helpful for stabilization purposes if these basic changes could be timed to coincide with stabilization needs. However, stabilization policies and programs must not be dependent on basic changes in tax and expenditure programs.

TAX POLICY CHANGES

What component of private demand should bear the brunt of fiscal adjustments to promote short-run stability? Should it be consumption or investment, and what kind of expenditures within these broad groups? It would be helpful if investment outlays could be pushed up in recessions and pulled down in booms, since they are the primary short-run destabilizer. Such a result would provide a more steady level of capital formation and more sustainable rate of growth. Yet this sector is probably more difficult to affect than any other. Consequently, it would appear that at present the best policy is to consider both investment and consumption as potential candidates for stabilization adjustments.

To be able to alter taxes or transfers for this purpose, they must meet certain criteria. Changes must be easy to make without creating uncertainty in the administration of, and compliance with, the tax law. They must be promptly effective and easily reversible. And they must not create uncertainty in business output, planning, and efficiency.

The personal income tax ranks high in satisfying these criteria, with cyclical varying of the starting rate preferable to varying personal exemptions. The tax is not a major factor in business planning; it is broadly based; and the rate can be easily varied and changes can take effect promptly through withholding. Variation in personal exemptions might create uncertainty from year to year for many taxpayers about whether they needed to file.

Excise taxes can be easily raised or lowered, but their initial effect on demand is perverse. Advance notice of changes must be given. Therefore, if rates are to be raised because demand is excessive, taxpayers are put on notice that their purchases will shortly cost them more. This encourages them to speed up purchases and increases demand. Similarly, if demand is deficient, a coming reduction in excise tax rates can lead to the postponement of purchases, further weakening demand. . . .

Temporary changes in social security contributions have some of the same advantages as changes in the starting rate of the personal income tax, but the employer contribution is a cost item and changes in it may disturb costs and prices. Furthermore, countercyclical variation in contributions may not be readily compatible with the nature of the old age insurance system; the government tries to maintain a schedule of contribution rates that matches actuarial estimates of costs in the long run. Also, the unemployment compensation system is state administered and might not be readily subject to variation. The federal payroll tax for unemployment compensation might be varied, with excess collections going into a federal fund to provide emergency relief in recessions.

Countercyclical adjustments in the corporation income tax rate, the remaining important tax to be considered, would almost surely create the most uncertainty for business. This holds for changes in the tax rate, as well as for changes in depreciation allowances or in investment credits.

As in the proposal for formula flexibility, the most appropriate choice for short-run discretionary changes in taxes is the first-bracket rate of the personal income tax. They are least likely to open up controversial questions of income tax structure. The legislative and administrative problems in making such changes would be relatively simple. No uncertainty would be encountered in complying with such changes. They could be made effective with very short notice to taxpayers through the withholding mechanism. They would be easily reversible. They would have a minimum of adverse side-effects such as causing uncertainty in business planning or speculation in commodities. Moreover, small changes in the tax rate would provide large amounts of additional spendable funds to consumers. A one-percentage point reduction in the tax rate would provide consumers with additional disposable income at an annual rate of well over $1 billion. . . .

If this rate reduction were expected to continue in effect for some time, the best evidence indicates that consumer expenditures would rise by a very large fraction of the increase in disposable income, probably by upwards of 80 cents on the dollar within a year of the date of tax reduction. In fact, more than half this response would probably occur in the first quarter following the tax reduction. It seems reasonable to suppose that the response in spending would be somewhat lower if the tax reduction were clearly understood to apply for only a brief period of six months or less, but almost no empirical evidence exists on which to base a quantitative estimate for such tax reductions. Conversely, tax increases would cause a fall in consumption as disposable income was reduced.

A variation of this procedure would be to make a percentage reduction in all rates and thus a percentage adjustment in final liabilities. In principle this is the same kind of device as a change in the starting rate alone, but it would apply to upper-brackets rates as well as to the starting rate.

Clearly, as a stabilization instrument, the first-bracket rate adjustment is superior to proportional adjustments in the entire rate structure in stimulating consumption, since for each dollar of income tax reduction the lower income groups would receive a proportionately larger share of the reductions.

The Commission therefore concludes that when discretionary tax adjustments are used to promote short-run economic stabilization, they should consist of variations in the first-bracket rate of the personal income tax.

Such variations should be regarded strictly as temporary departures from a permanent tax structure. Under such a plan the starting rate could be shifted to a temporary level, either up or down, for as long a period as is believed desirable, with a corresponding adjustment provided in the final tax liabilities for the year depending upon the length of time over which the temporary rate was in effect. For example, if the first-bracket rate were cut two percentage points to 18 percent for six months, the annual liability would be based on a 19 percent starting rate, rather than on the present annual rate of 20 percent. Obviously, there are many possible variants of this illustration.

The main point to emphasize here is that short-run stabilization adjustments are not the place to make basic changes in the tax structure. The permanent rate structure should be governed by such considerations as tax equity, investment incentives, and economic growth. Full consideration of all these factors is not really relevant to this section on short-run stabilization policy.

Because of the vicissitudes attending the consideration of ordinary legislation, the President's responsibilities for prompt and decisive action under the Employment Act warrant a limited delegation of power to initiate a tax rate change as an instrument of countercyclical fiscal policy. Any proposal to vest the President with stand-by power to alter tax rates for any reason under any circumstances runs counter to the long-established tradition, jealously guarded, that gives the House Ways and Means Committee exclusive jurisdiction to originate revenue measures. The Congress since 1934, to be sure, has acquiesced in a delegation of power to the President, within specified limits and conditions, to change tariff rates under the Reciprocal Trade Agreements Acts, but only because tariffs vitally affect our foreign policy—traditionally a primary concern of the President, and a field in which he is otherwise accorded a wide latitude of discretion—and because the trade agreements can hardly be negotiated without the offer of firm commitments. Even in this case the Ways and Means Committee, not the Committee on Foreign Affairs, initiated the basic legislation.

The delegation should specify the particular rate to be changed and limit the maximum amount and duration of the changes, as well as the conditions under which it is to be made. Finally, the delegation should be accompanied by an opportunity for a congressional veto of its application in particular cases, along lines currently employed when executive reorganization plans are authorized. This procedure protects the opportunity for timely action by assuring that a tax adjustment, once formally proposed, will not get lost in a shuffle of alternative proposals; it must be acted upon, in the form submitted, within a limited time. Moreover, it minimizes the disturbance in the balance of executive-legislative power.

The position of the Commission on discretionary changes in tax rates is summarized below.

1. One obstacle to stabilizing tax policy has been the failure to disassociate temporary and reversible changes for stabilization purposes from permanent and structural changes. It is the Commission's view that techniques must be developed by which tax policy can be applied more flexibly, and that the first step in this direction lies in the separation of short-run cyclical tax changes from long-run structural changes in the tax system.

2. Among various alternative taxes, the personal income tax lends itself best to countercyclical variation, and adjustments in the first-bracket rate are recommended as the best type of change.

3. In order to provide maximum flexibility for stabilizing tax changes, the Commission recommends that Congress grant to the President limited conditional power to make temporary countercyclical adjustments in the first-bracket rate of the personal in-

come tax, the grant to be accompanied by the following qualifications and safeguards:

(*a*) The power should be available for exercise only when the President has issued a statement that in his judgment economic conditions are running significantly counter to the objectives set forth in the Employment Act as amended.

(*b*) The range of permissible adjustment should be limited to five percentage points upward or downward, that is, one-quarter of the present 20 percent rate.

(*c*) The duration of the adjustment should be limited to six months subject to renewal by the same process, unless Congress acts sooner by law to extend or supplant it.

(*d*) The exercise of the conditional power by the President should be subject to a legislative veto by a concurrent resolution of both houses of Congress before any tax adjustment takes effect, in accordance with the procedures made familiar by the recent Reorganization Acts. To this end the President should be required to lay before the Congress any proposal to adjust the tax rate, the proposal to lie there up to 60 days, unless a concurrent resolution of disapproval is sooner voted on and rejected, and to take effect only if no such resolution is adopted in that time. In the same law that authorizes the adjustment, the parliamentary rules of the two houses should be amended ad hoc in a manner to ensure that a concurrent resolution of disapproval may be introduced and voted upon within a 60-day period.

The Federal Tax Cut and the Economy

ARTHUR F. BURNS

Professor Burns weighed the effects of the 1964 tax cut and set forth a proposal for annual tax reductions in this address delivered at Oregon State University in June 1964.

THE PASSAGE of the tax bill earlier this year represents the culmination of efforts by many citizens to bring about a revision of our tax system. A revision was long overdue.

The tax system that we still had at the beginning of this year was a legacy of the Great Depression and of the war that followed. During the 1930s, when many of our workshops were idle and much of our industrial equipment was only partly used, there was little public interest in encouraging industrial research or investment. Our national effort during those difficult years was concentrated on stimulating consumer spending and on economic and social reforms. The federal tax system played a large part in this policy. By 1936 taxes on personal incomes in the higher brackets had already risen sharply, with the maximum marginal rate reaching 79 percent. The maximum rate under the estate tax was lifted to 70 percent, while exemptions were reduced. A new gift tax was enacted with a maximum rate of 52½ percent. Of course, the tax rate on corporate income also went up. The outbreak of World War II led to still stiffer federal taxation of high personal incomes and of corporate incomes. Not only that but taxes for individuals were raised over the entire income scale and personal exemptions were drastically lowered, so that millions of individuals of modest means were brought under the income tax.

In the postwar period, various revisions of federal taxes were made—some downward as during 1948 and 1954, one upward during the Korean war. However, the broad features of our federal tax system at the beginning of this year were still much the same as they were in 1945. The personal income tax started with a rate of 20 percent and rose to 91 percent for very high income brackets. Exemptions were low, merely $600 per person. The basic corporate tax rate stood at 52 percent. And while federal taxes were practically maintained at wartime levels, state and local taxes—on property, on consumer purchases, on incomes— kept rising steadily during the postwar period. The result was that a rather large and increasing part of the substance drawn from personal and business efforts was being diverted to government.

How large the tax burden had become is conveyed by the fact that the revenues collected by government at all levels (federal, state, and local) amounted in 1963 to $169 billion. Since our gross national product in that year was $585 billion, taxes came to about 29 percent of the gross national product. Once we take account of depreciation in reckoning output, as indeed we should, it may fairly be said that taxes in 1963 took about one-third of the nation's total production of goods and services. Not only had the tax burden become very heavy, but our taxes were in large part levied on the earnings of individuals and of business firms rather than on consumption. We went further in this respect than did other nations.

While our federal tax system stood nearly still during the postwar years, other nations displayed considerable imagination and enterprise in changing their modes of taxation. Throughout the postwar period Germany, Japan, and other industrial countries kept redesigning their tax systems in the interest of stimulating enterprise, innovation, and investment. The brilliant economic successes of Western Europe and Japan excited our interest in their tax programs, and this interest became more intense as the growth rate of our economy continued to lag. Reformers in our midst urged tax reform and tax reduction, and they won powerful allies among business executives and labor leaders. A serious debate on fiscal problems got under way and its outcome is the tax legislation passed by the Congress this year.

The main features of the new federal tax law can be summarized briefly. First, the initial rate under the personal income tax is lowered from 20 to 14 percent, while the maximum rate is reduced from 91 to 70 percent. Second, the basic rate of the corporate income tax is lowered from 52 to 48 percent. Third, these changes in tax liability are to be carried out partly this year and partly next year. Fourth, the provisions with regard to withholding are such that personal payments under the income tax are being reduced more rapidly this year than are personal tax liabilities. As a result, the tax reduction for individuals, viewed in the aggregate, has already been accomplished. Fifth, the overall reduction of taxes for both individuals and corporations amounts to $11½ billion when estimated on the basis of 1963 incomes. Of this figure, approximately $9 billion represents a reduction of personal income taxes, and the remaining $2½ billion represents a reduction of corporate income taxes. In connection with corporations, however, it should be noted that many of them had already benefited from the investment tax credit which the Congress legislated in 1962, as well as from the new depreciation guidelines that the Treasury promulgated in the same year.

Let me turn now to the results that may be expected from the new tax legislation. One probable result is some curbing of the growth of federal expenditures. In order to persuade the House of Representatives to pass the tax bill, President Kennedy promised, in effect, that federal expenditures would henceforth be controlled more tightly than in the recent past. President Johnson has carried the move to frugality further. Whether President Johnson's budget truly represents a reduction of $1 billion in federal expenditures during fiscal year 1965 is debatable. I, for one, do not think it does. But whatever view one may take on the question whether the direction of federal spending is still upward, it is a fact that the rate of increase in federal spending has recently been significantly curtailed. Furthermore, it would be reasonable to expect that the Congress, mindful of the sizable deficit in the federal budget, will strive somewhat harder to curb expenditures in the years immediately ahead than it has in the recent past.

The larger question, of course, is what effects the tax reduction may have on the rate of our nation's economic activity. Since the reduction has been in effect only since the middle of March, its direct benefits thus far have necessarily been small. However, it is well to recall that President Kennedy's proposal to reduce both corporate and personal income taxes was first publicly made in the early fall of 1962. In the year and a half that followed, more and more citizens came to feel that a substantial tax reduction would actually take place. The growing expectation of a tax cut undoubtedly stimulated some individuals to spend more boldly and likewise encouraged some business firms to plan—or even to undertake—larger investments in new plant and equipment. In a complicated economy such as ours, taxes are merely one factor in the economic equation. This cannot be overemphasized. Still, it seems clear that the growing expectation of tax reduction served to increase the confidence of people in the economic future and thereby contributed to the economic upsurge during the past year.

But what of the months and years ahead? Taking the long view, the paramount fact is that the recent legislation has reduced the drag of the tax system on economic activity. As a result of the tax cut, economic incentives to work and to invest will be stronger. Also, the financial wherewithal of individuals and of business firms—especially of the smaller enterprises—will tend to be larger. But although it seems clear that the tax cut will prove beneficial to our economy over the long run, prudence requires that we recognize that over the next year or two the tax cut may prove to be a mixed blessing.

To explain what I mean, let me call your attention to several facts about our national economy that are presently of large significance. First, the economy is generally prosperous and is continuing the advance that got under way early in 1961. Production is at a record high level. So, too, is the volume of employment, the flow of income to individuals, and the volume of aggregate spending by business, individuals, and government. The rate of unemployment, which has recently fallen to 5.1 percent, is still too high—but this figure requires some interpretation. The unemployment rate for married men, who constitute the hard core of the labor force, has fallen to 2.6 percent—which is about the level that we experienced during the boom year of 1956. Lately, overtime work in manufacturing has been more extensive than ever, and the same appears to be true of moonlighting—that is, of the number of dual jobholders. Much of our unemployment is concentrated among young people, most of whom are unskilled and many of whom are being priced out of the labor market by existing wage levels.

A second outstanding fact about our national economy at present is that profits are rising. Profit margins have recently experienced a strong improvement. . . . With profit margins widening and the physical volume of business sales growing, aggregate profits have of late been rising handsomely. This improvement, while not universal, is widely diffused over our economy.

Let me note a third outstanding fact. The margins of excess industrial capacity in our economy have been narrowing. In some industries—for example, the aluminum industry, the paper industry, and various branches of the chemicals industry—excess industrial capacity has virtually disappeared. Moreover, much of what we sometimes speak of as excess capacity of industry is obsolete and should not be viewed as a serious deterrent to investment. Early this year the Department of Commerce asked manufacturers to evaluate their productive capacity in the light of current and prospective sales during 1964. Only 9 percent of manufacturing firms reported that their existing plant and equipment exceeded needs. On the other hand, 32 percent reported that they would require additional fixed capital. The latter group, taking account of size, accounts for half of manufacturing industry.

A fourth outstanding fact about the current economy is that money is readily available and can be borrowed upon favorable terms from financial institutions. During the past year the money supply, defined narrowly to include only demand deposits and currency in public circulation, rose 4 percent. The money supply defined more broadly, so as to include also time deposits of commercial banks, rose 8 percent. To be sure, during the past year the free reserves of commercial banks have shrunk and some money-market rates of interest have risen. However, no rise at all has occurred in interest rates on mortgages. This highly important type of interest rate is as low as it has been at any time during the past four or five years. The like is true of yields on medium grade bonds and of interest rates charged by commercial banks to their over-the-counter customers. Our financial institutions are still engaged in very keen competition, and they continue to hunt customers eagerly.

The final fact to which I want to call your attention is that optimism has spread and is now running strong in our nation. Businessmen appear to be more optimistic now than they have been at any time since 1956. By and large, they are optimistic about the future of their own businesses and about the future of the nation's economy. They are less concerned about international relations, and apparently feel that an era of peace lies ahead. Of late, many businessmen have even become optimistic about the trend and character of federal economic policies, and not a few speak with admiration of the economic thinking that emanates from the White House.

In view of these major facts—the continuing advance of production and employment, the strong improvement of profits, the gradual disappearance of excess industrial capacity, the continuance of easy conditions in the money market, and the spread of optimism—it would appear that our national economy may well be on the threshold of a boom. . . .

I cannot stop to elaborate the statistical picture of our economy. But perhaps I have said enough to indicate the broad economic setting in which a massive tax cut has just become effective. Of late, our economy has been advancing with considerable vigor. This does not mean that the tax cut was unwise. On the contrary, as I have already argued, it should prove beneficial to our nation over the long run. In view of current conditions, however, it would have been better to spread the tax cut more or less evenly over two or three years, instead of largely concentrating it in this year.

There is some danger that the tax cut, coming when it did and on the scale that it has, may for a while over-stimulate the economy: that it may lead to a renewal of inflation or expectations thereof, to speculation in inventories, to over-building of industrial facilities, perhaps even to an extension of the over-building that has already occurred in many places of office structures, apartment houses, and hotels. If events took this turn, hard times would probably follow. Not only that but, if a recession were to occur next year, it could be more serious than earlier recessions of the postwar period.

Let me point to one reason why this might happen. If a recession occurred in 1965, it would start from a position of sizable deficit in the federal budget. After the recession had run a few months, the reduction of tax liabilities would cause the deficit to rise sharply, and we might then face a deficit of something like 15 or 20 billion dollars. At a time such as that, economic and political thinking in our country being what it is, any proposal to cut taxes again with a view to countering the recession would not meet with favor, first, because of the very magnitude of the deficit and, second, because many people would be disillusioned about the economic effectiveness of tax cuts. In other words, if a recession occurred next year, the Congress would not be inclined to legislate another tax cut and it might even drag its heels on federal spending. The cure of the recession would therefore need to depend heavily on natural processes of recovery which, as history teaches us, sometimes work very slowly. Another way of saying what I have tried to convey is that the recent tax cut has reduced the likelihood of effective contracyclical policy in the event of an early recession. On the other hand, if the current expansion stretches out another two or three years the vitality of our present contracyclical tools will be restored and even enhanced. The importance of extending our current prosperity is therefore very great.

The government can minimize the danger that I have depicted by restraining the growth of credit, and I believe that a modest step in this direction would be salutary. We have had an extraordinary expansion of debt, and probably also some decline of its quality, in the last few years. This has been accompanied by a rapid increase in the money supply—an increase that has not yet worked out its full economic effects. The stock of liquid assets held by the public, which rose at an average annual rate of about $13 billion between 1955 and 1960, increased by $25 billion in 1961, by $34 billion in 1962, and by $36 billion in 1963. When money is once created on an abundant scale, we can be reasonably sure that it will go places. Of late, money has gone rather exuberantly into the stock market and has sent prices soaring in that sector of our economy. Before long, if the recent rate of expansion of the money supply continues, there is a fair probability that commodity prices will begin rising significantly. We must not overlook the fact that prices of raw materials have already risen perceptibly, that prices of manufactured products have begun stirring in an upward direction, and that increases of wage rates appear to be accelerating somewhat. If my way of thinking about our national economy is valid, then some restraint on the growth of credit would help our nation to derive the maximum potential benefit from the recent reduction of tax rates.

Before concluding, I should like to express the hope that the recent tax law may prove to be the first step in a long-range, continuing process of tax reduction. Our federal tax system is highly productive of revenue. When our economy grows at something like a normal rate, it is reasonable to expect that the existing structure of tax rates will add about five or six billion dollars a year to federal revenues. This means that we could reduce tax rates every year, or nearly every year, and still have sufficient revenues to meet any modest increases in federal spending that may be needed. I can think of no policy that is better designed to stimulate the growth of our economy than a continuing policy of modest, year-by-year reductions of tax rates. This is, in effect, what Japan has done in the postwar period, and the policy has worked remarkably well in that country. The policy that I speak of implies, of course, that the growth of federal expenditures will be curbed effectively.

In another two or three years, if the federal budget is again approximately in balance, we will be able as a people to embark prudently on a systematic program of annual tax reductions. But in order to do that, plans will have to be worked out in some detail, and we will need to strive for a national consensus on the issue. I very much hope that many economists will join in the enterprise of molding a truly long-range tax policy, whether along the lines that I have suggested or along some other line. I am convinced that our national tax burden is still too high. Revisions of the tax structure as well as systematic rate reductions will be needed to enable our economy to flourish and advance as it both can and should.

The Tax-cut Harvest

JAMES TOBIN

James Tobin is Sterling Professor of Economics at Yale University. He was a member of President Kennedy's Council of Economic Advisers in 1961–1962. This selection appeared in The New Republic in March 1964, shortly after enactment of the 1964 tax reduction.

THE TAX CUT represents our first deliberate major use of the federal budget for stimulation of the economy. It is thus an historic event. At a time when the budget is already in substantial deficit, the President and the Congress are cutting taxes $11.5 billion a year.

Liberals should give credit where it is due. Ever since Keynes, they have argued that the budget should be manipulated to balance the economy at full employment—against the orthodox view that the economy should be sacrificed to balance the budget every year. The Employment Act of 1946 seemed to declare a national consensus that federal fiscal and monetary powers should be employed to stabilize the economy and prevent unemployment. But this consensus, always fragile, eroded during the 1950s when orthodox financial sermons were repeatedly preached from the Presidential pulpit. Budget deficits we had nonetheless, but they were for the most part the unplanned consequence of economic weakness. Now at long last a planned deficit is accepted to gain economic strength.

Satisfaction with this victory should not, I think, be appreciably dimmed by the evident fact that tax reduction has been supported for a mixture of motives and justified by a variety of arguments. There is not a Keynesian majority in Congress, and conscious deficit finance is still not respectable. But actions speak louder than words. The country and the Congress accepted the view of Presidents Kennedy and Johnson that the economic pump needed priming, and that a tax cut was the way to prime it.

The tax cut has been purchased, it is true, by some reduction in the federal budget. By holding administrative budget expenditures for fiscal year 1965 within the 1964 figure, President Johnson secured early passage of a bill which might otherwise have been passed, if at all, only after economically dangerous delay. We can only applaud his political acumen while regretting the misguided but powerful ideology which made his bargain necessary. How large and how permanent a reduction of federal expenditure has been made because of the tax cut is a different historical conjecture. So far budgetary frugality appears to be wiping out less than a third of the fiscal stimulus of the full tax reduction.

The main savings are in defense, which had been built up substantially under President Kennedy to remedy strategic weaknesses and to deal with crises in Berlin, Vietnam, and Cuba. We cannot really complain if now Secretary McNamara's efficiency experts and a cold war *détente* combine to stabilize or reduce defense expenditures. President Johnson is right to scorn both a nuclear WPA and obsolete bases.

The President's declared war on poverty begins modestly, with only $500 million in the new budget. But a serious, well-organized campaign will need much more, and will in time learn how to spend it fruitfully. In recent sessions of Congress, spending to meet America's social needs has not been popular; the "war on poverty" may turn out, however, to be the banner under which is mobilized political support for causes that have been short-changed. If so, the longer-run prospects for federal expenditures, both in size and in direction, are not disheartening. Moreover, one effect of federal tax reduction is to increase the politically feasible tax base of states and localities, which can be counted on to spend new tax receipts for education and other urgent social needs.

The main purpose of the tax cut is to reduce unemployment. The difference between an unemployment rate of 5.5 percent of the labor force and a rate of 4 percent corresponds to a deficiency of about $30 billion a year or 5 percent in total national spending, public and private, for goods and services. To produce $30 billion extra in goods and services, American business would have to give jobs to about 30 percent of the manpower now unemployed, and put to work a corresponding amount of idle industrial plant capacity.

The gap in demand and production has remained about the same over the past two years. Yet total national spending has been increasing 5 percent per year. The economy has to run forward at that pace just to stay in the same place. A 5 percent annual increase in the Gross National Product suffices only to absorb the normal increases in the labor force, in labor productivity and in prices. It leaves the unemployment rate undiminished. To eliminate the $30 billion gap, spending needs to increase by 7 or 8 percent for a couple of years.

How can a tax reduction of $11.5 billion a year add $30 billion to total demand? The key point is that we need to find only half of the required $30 billion; if we can do that, the other half will take care of itself. In the normal course of events, an increase of $30 billion in production and income would by itself generate about $15 billion in additional consumer spending—the other $15 billion going into personal and corporate tax payments and savings. Observe, for example, that the $100 billion increase in GNP from the first quarter of 1961 to the last quarter of 1963 led to a $50 billion increase in consumer spending—a result just of the growth of personal incomes, without any help from tax cuts or other measures to stimulate consumption.

The $11.5 billion tax reduction, when it is fully in effect, can be expected to increase consumer spending by $9 billion; this estimate takes account of the allocation of the benefits between corporations and individuals and among individual taxpayers in various brackets. To make up the full $30 billion, then, requires $6 billion more in nonconsumer spending. To provide this, government and business spending together must not only keep pace with the normal growth of the economy but increase further by about 1 percent of GNP.

INCREASE IN BUSINESS SPENDING

The major reliance must be on business expenditures for new plant and equipment. To restore full employment they must grow from 8.5 percent of full employment GNP, as they have been running recently, to 9.5 percent. Indeed, they must rise a bit more than that, perhaps to 10 percent, in order to make up for the prospective slowdown in the growth of federal expenditures. There is a reasonable chance that this will happen, though not all in one year. Business fixed investment has been weak in recent years that have been characterized by excess capacity and economic slack, but it typically exceeded 10 percent of GNP in earlier periods of prosperity, both postwar and pre-war. Business investment plans for 1964 are cautious, but there is evidence that they are already being revised upward. The year 1964 may well set the stage for a spurt in investment in 1965. The profit and liquidity positions of business are already favorable, and they are reinforced by the tax incentives for investment introduced by the Kennedy and Johnson administrations. With consumer spending boosted by the tax cut, demand may rise enough in 1964 to cut down excess capacity. This will add the strategic investment incentive that has so far been missing throughout much of American industry, the need to build new capacity to meet expanding demand.

For this prospect we have to thank the wisdom of the Administration and Congress in deciding to cut the withholding rate four points right away, instead of three points now and one in 1965 as originally planned. For 1964 this revision in plans more than compensates for President Johnson's frugality. The timing has been criticized by some who fear it overstimulates the economy in 1964 and by others who fear the absence of sufficient new stimulus in 1965. But the timing appears to be excellent economic strategy. [In 1964], while business investment is still cautious, the economy needs all the stimulus to consumer spending which the tax cut can provide. [In 1965], with the pump well primed, business investment should keep the economy moving ahead.

One cloud on this horizon is monetary policy. Some monetary officials are inclined to view the tax cut not as a measure to expand demand faster but as a reason to tighten credit further. Worried more about inflation than unemployment, they are constitutionally disposed to jitters about economic booms. Moreover, their European fraternity brothers keep telling them that a country with a balance-of-payments deficit, like the United States, should have higher interests rates. As the President and Congress release the fiscal brakes on the economy, they may feel freer to step on the monetary brakes. The Administration will have to be alert to prevent the tax cut from being wasted in higher interest rates.

TAXES AND THE IMPOVERISHED

Like most major legislative proposals, the tax cut has probably been overadvertised. To repeat, its essential purpose is to reduce unemployment, to eliminate the waste of manpower and productive capacity that has plagued our economy for the past six years. That is enough to justify it, and enough to expect of it. Tax reduction will not by itself solve all our other economic problems. Let us consider its relationship to three of these problems: the balance-of-payments deficit, the long-run of economic growth, and poverty.

On the balance of payments, the tax cut has no direct impact, and it is hard to predict its indirect effects. On the one hand, a more prosperous domestic economy will import more. On the other hand, profitable operation at full capacity may keep wayward investment funds at home. Another possibility is the one mentioned above, that the Federal Reserve will respond to the tax cut by raising interest rates in order to attract internationally mobile liquid funds. If so, the tax cut can be said to be good for the balance of payments only at the expense of some of its benefits for the domestic economy and domestic investment.

The tax cut has been billed as a measure to promote economic growth. And, true enough, as its stimulus helps the economy recover lost ground, GNP and other statistics will show higher year-to-year "growth" rates for a time. For the central purpose of the measure is precisely to restore full capacity operation of the economy. But a more meaningful measure of "growth" is the rate at which the economy's capacity itself grows. This, over the long pull, is the trend that determines how fast standards of living rise.

The tax cut is good for long-run growth only in the general sense that prosperity is good for investment. And, as observed above, the main kind of spending that the tax cut stimulates is consumption. Growth would have been better served if the same increase in spending could have taken the form of public or private investments. But a large increase in public investment was not possible politically, and a large enough increase in private investment may not have been feasible economically. It surely would have required an aggressive and persistent easy-money policy—probably unthinkable to our monetary leaders in the best of circumstances and certainly out of the question when their primary aim was to defend the gold stock.

As for poverty, a dose of demand stimulant is necessary but by no means sufficient medicine. So long as there is a general shortage of jobs, the war on poverty will be an uphill battle. Those who suffer most from high national unemployment—Negroes, teenagers, workers lacking skills, experience, literacy, or education, workers in depressed areas—have the most to gain from full employment. Sustained general prosperity will not by itself solve their difficult problems, but it will make them much less intractable. Specific programs of education, training and retraining, area redevelopment, equal opportunity and urban rehabilitation are certainly essential. But they are doomed to considerable frustration so long as national spending is inadequate and jobs are scarce; there is little point in shifting poverty and unemployment from group to group or region to region. If the campaign is to be a *national* success, it needs desperately a favorable *national* economic climate.

It should be said that the cut comes too late, in the sense that the economy would be in better shape today if taxes had been reduced two or three or even six years ago. In January, 1961, the Samuelson committee, one of President-elect Kennedy's pre-inauguration task forces, suggested that serious consideration be given to a temporary tax cut to help bring the economy out of recession. This suggestion was not implemented, partly because the recovery that began promptly after the inauguration proceeded vigorously throughout 1961, partly because the balanced budget fetish was still very powerful.

(In January, 1962, President Kennedy proposed, as anti-recession insurance, new procedures for making quick, temporary, pre-fabricated cuts in tax rates. The proposal caused scarcely a ripple in Congress, but it deserves to be revived. If Congress needs 15 months to enact a tax bill, tax adjustments are not very useful weapons against cyclical recessions or inflations.)

By the summer of 1962, it was clear that the recovery was faltering. The idea of a tax cut, perhaps temporary, perhaps permanent, was revived. President Kennedy announced in mid-August that he had decided against it, but at the same time he committed the Administration to offer a major proposal for permanent tax reduction and reform in January, 1963. The idea of a 1962 tax cut had not evoked much enthusiasm in public or Congressional opinion. Indeed, the business and financial community rather mysteriously backed away from the favorable stand taken earlier in the summer by the Chamber of Commerce. Moreover, the Treasury had its heart set on tax reform and believed that the interested parties would swallow the bitter pills of reforms only with a thick sugar-coating of tax reduction. In retrospect, it is clear that this strategy failed. The Congress removed the bitter pills of reform from the candy anyway. The tax cut should have taken the form of a quick, simple, neutral, uniform, across-the-board reduction in rates, leaving revision of the tax structure for later and longer deliberation. The attempt to obtain reform served only to delay the Administration's proposal and its enactment by Congress.

Broadly considered, two kinds of reform were at stake. One was to enlarge the base of the personal income tax, eliminating or limiting special deductions from taxable income and substituting lower rates. The other was to plug some of the many loopholes through which high-income taxpayers escape the high rates to which they are nominally subject, in return moderating the progressiveness of the rate structure. For the most part Congress provided lower and less progressive rates without broadening the tax base or eliminating loopholes. Thus the whole episode cost the cause of tax reform a good deal of its bargaining power.

The bill just passed, though good economics and a victory for rational fiscal policy, is not the last word on federal taxes. Real reform still lies ahead. And economic circumstances in the future may require either higher or still lower rates than those now enacted. The history of this legislation indicates that we in the United States still have much to learn in making taxation a flexible and responsive instrument of economic stabilization.

PART FOUR

Monetary Policy

The Influence of Monetary Policy on
Economic Stability
BOARD OF GOVERNORS, FEDERAL RESERVE SYSTEM

*This official explanation of how monetary policy works is part
of the Board of Governors' publication,* The Federal Reserve
System: Purposes and Functions. *Ralph A. Young, adviser to the
Board, supervised the staff efforts in preparing the publication.*

RESERVE BANKING policy attempts to provide a financial climate
conducive to sustainable growth in output, employment, and
consumption under conditions of relative stability in the average level of prices and of long-run balance in our international
payments. However, these objectives cannot be attained through
reliance on monetary policy alone. Their accomplishment also
depends on fiscal and other governmental policies and on policies
of private institutions and organizations.

The posture of Federal Reserve monetary policy at any moment—whether restrictive or expansive—is a reaction to prevailing economic conditions. Monetary policy functions restrictively
when inflationary tendencies are present. In other circumstances
it functions expansively or assumes a posture somewhere between stimulation and restraint. To help avoid the dangers of
economic downturn, reserve banking works to prevent speculative or otherwise unsustainable expansion of bank credit.

The diagram on the following page shows in a simplified way
how actions taken by the Federal Reserve System influence total
spending and thereby contribute to the ultimate objectives of
high employment, maximum production, and stable prices.

The Federal Reserve carries out its responsibility for the public interest by influencing the reserves of member banks. As
the diagram shows, that is where the initial impact of reserve
banking policy falls. As banks respond to changes in the avail-

FLOW OF FEDERAL RESERVE INFLUENCE

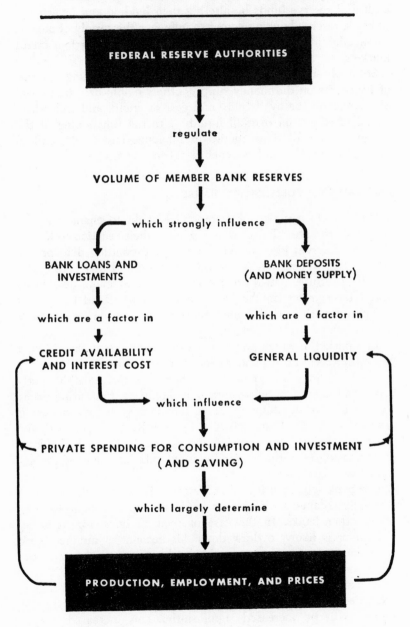

FEDERAL RESERVE AUTHORITIES

regulate

VOLUME OF MEMBER BANK RESERVES

which strongly influence

BANK LOANS AND
INVESTMENTS

BANK DEPOSITS
(AND MONEY SUPPLY)

which are a factor in

which are a factor in

CREDIT AVAILABILITY
AND INTEREST COST

GENERAL LIQUIDITY

which influence

PRIVATE SPENDING FOR CONSUMPTION AND INVESTMENT
(AND SAVING)

which largely determine

PRODUCTION, EMPLOYMENT, AND PRICES

ability of reserve funds by altering their lending and investment policies, reserve banking comes to influence the supply of money, the availability of credit, and the cost of money in various credit markets.

Some observers stress the influence of reserve banking in terms of its effects on the money supply, others emphasize the impact of changes in the availability and cost of credit, and still others stress its effects on over-all liquidity. In the functioning of the economy each of these modes of influence has a role, and in the discussion that follows each is taken into account.

REACTIONS OF COMMERCIAL BANKS

What is the reaction of commercial banks to changes in the supply of reserves? For example, what is their reaction to limitations on reserves in a period of strongly expanding demand for bank loans? When they are in this situation and therefore under reserve pressure, banks are more reluctant to make new loans and interest rates on the loans they do make tend to rise, as compared with periods when their reserves are rising rapidly as the result of reserve banking policy.

In a period in which policy is limiting bank credit expansion, a bank that seeks to expand its loans rapidly may have to obtain funds by selling Government or other securities (mainly short-term) in the market, by permitting its holdings of maturing issues to run off, or by drawing down balances with, or borrowing from, other banks. Discounting at Reserve Banks, is primarily for meeting passing contingencies and is not, in the U.S. banking system, a source of funds to individual banks for financing permanent loan expansion.

If a bank sells securities, lets maturing issues run off, or draws down its balance with another bank, its action will necessarily affect other banks. In the case of security sales, for example, the buyer is likely to draw down his account at another bank to make payment. Consequently, banks as a group cannot expand their total loans and investments in this way.

If many banks try to obtain additional reserves by selling securities, the amount of short-term paper or securities in the market will be increased significantly. This increased supply tends to lower prices and to raise yields on all such paper. Similar market pressures may result if banks, in order to build up their reserves, allow maturing issues to run off or draw upon balances with correspondents.

At the lower prices and higher yields, Government and other short-term securities will be more attractive. In order to buy them, nonbank investors may use temporarily idle deposits or they may even be induced to economize on cash balances held for current payments. When banks sell short-term paper to other investors and use the proceeds to make loans, ownership of deposits may shift from holders of idle balances to borrowers who are spenders and will shortly disburse the proceeds. To the extent that this occurs, the velocity of existing deposits will increase. In this process, the volume of money transactions increases as the existing supply of money is used more actively.

As banks see their short-term securities or secondary reserves declining, however, they become increasingly reluctant to reduce these securities or reserves further in order to make additional loans. This leads banks to raise interest rates on loans and to adopt more selective loan standards.

In addition, as market interest rates rise—a development that is reinforced by bank sales of securities—security prices decline and sales of securities may involve book losses. Banks are influenced to some extent by potential capital losses on the securities in their portfolios, and they hesitate to sell securities at a loss. Income tax considerations and strict earnings calculations, however, may moderate or even negate the deterrent effect of such losses on continued sales of securities.

At times when monetary policy aims at stimulating bank credit expansion to help counteract recessionary tendencies in the economy, banks will find their reserve funds increasing quite rapidly. In using these funds, they are likely first to repay any outstanding indebtedness to the Reserve Banks, particularly if loan demands are weak or declining as might be expected under the conditions assumed. After they have reduced their borrowings, banks will begin to purchase short-term securities, thereby rebuilding their secondary reserve positions and reinforcing any tendency already existing in the market toward declining interest rates. They will also begin to relax their loan policies and this, together with reduced interest rates, may actively encourage the extension of bank loans that were postponed or that were not encouraged by lenders under the earlier conditions of credit restraint.

EFFECTS OF CHANGES IN THE MONEY SUPPLY

Changes in bank reserve availability influence changes in the money supply. What is the response of the economy to changes in the rate at which the supply of money is growing, under the influence of monetary policy?

At each level of income and interest rates, there will be an amount of money that the public wishes to hold for transactions, or for precautionary or speculative purposes. Suppose that actions taken by the Federal Reserve fail to provide the desired amount of money. In that event some reaction is likely to be registered both in spending and in interest rates.

In an attempt to reestablish its desired level of balances, the public may spend less, or it may sell off financial assets (or purchase fewer of them), with a consequent rise in interest rates. As interest rates rise in this situation, they too influence decisions to spend and to save. Also, the rise in interest rates affects the demand for money balances, as it leads people to accommodate themselves to smaller cash balances.

On the other hand, a volume of money in excess of what the public wishes to hold leads to increased spending and lending and to reductions in interest rates.

Demand for Cash · In assessing the effect on economic activity of changes in the money supply, it is important to recognize that there is no simple automatic measure of the appropriate relationship between the amount of money outstanding and the level of economic activity. A given volume of money, for example, can be associated with either higher or lower levels of total spending—that is, can finance more or fewer transactions—depending on how often it is used. The rate of turnover, or velocity, of money indicates how much work each unit of money does in financing transactions.

Cash balances are held by private sectors of the economy for a variety of reasons. A large part of their total represents working balances, that is, amounts of demand deposits and currency held for financing regular transactions. The size of such balances varies in part with the time lag between receipts and expenditures. For example, the time that elapses between pay dates is one factor affecting the size of cash balances. People who are paid every week have smaller cash balances, on the average, than those who are paid monthly. The size of the cash balance also varies with income. The higher a person's income and expenditures, the larger his cash balance for transactions is likely to be.

Cash balances are held for other reasons too. They may represent saving out of income, as a store of value for precautionary reasons—to gain flexibility in choice and timing of purchases, to provide against a rainy day, or to anticipate future expenditures or investments. In other instances they may be held as a store of value for speculative reasons, with the expectation of buying in case of a sharp decline in security, real estate, or commodity prices.

The size of the cash balances that businesses and individuals find it desirable to hold depends in part on the level of interest rates. When interest rates are low, the holder sacrifices relatively little in holding cash rather than an asset that earns interest. The higher the level of interest rates, the greater the sacrifice in holding idle cash instead of an interest-bearing financial asset. The form in which contingency or speculative balances are held —whether it be in demand deposits that bear no interest or in interest-earning assets—is highly sensitive to the rate of interest paid.

Several types of assets are close substitutes for cash in its store-of-value function. These include savings and time deposits at commercial banks, deposits at mutual savings banks, shares in savings and loan associations, and U.S. Government savings bonds. Short-term market instruments, especially obligations of the U.S. Government, such as Treasury bills, are also close substitutes for cash because they are generally convertible into cash with relatively small risk of capital loss. Such assets possess high, though varying, degrees of liquidity. A backlog of these "near money" assets, together with some holdings of cash, gives the individual consumer or enterprise greater discretion in making its decisions to spend.

Use of Cash in Relation to Monetary Policy · Efforts of reserve banking policy to curb inflationary spending by limiting expansion of the money supply are generally accompanied by more active use of cash balances by the public. Some individuals and businesses may increase their spending by drawing upon their own existing cash balances or by converting financial assets into cash. As interest rates rise in this situation, others will be induced to put their idle balances to work in interest-earning assets. Such an addition to the flow of available credit tends to offset somewhat the credit-restraining effects of anti-inflationary monetary policy.

As incomes rise in an expansionary period, however, people will feel a growing need for transactions cash, and it will become increasingly inconvenient for them to economize on existing holdings. For this reason many economists believe that a rise in velocity in this situation will approach a definable limit. Another reason is that there are limits to the increases in interest rates that nonbank financial institutions can offer to induce the public to economize on cash holdings. Institutions are limited in bidding for funds because when they pay higher interest rates this affects the cost of their lending, and as lending costs rise borrowing becomes less attractive to businesses and individuals. Therefore, the ability of institutions to attract funds and to use them profitably is reduced.

When economic activity is declining, efforts to stimulate spending by encouraging expansion of the money supply may be accompanied by a less active use of cash balances. The expansionary effects of additions to bank reserves and the supply of money may be weakened, in other words, by a rise, however activated, in the public's desire to hold cash and by an accompanying decline in the velocity of money. As a result, countercyclical monetary action, even though aggressive, may not be accompanied by a commensurate rise in spending.

With the changing use of cash balances a potential countervailing force to monetary policy, it is necessarily incumbent on the monetary authorities to pay close attention to money velocity and to weigh its strength carefully in determining possible actions.

EFFECT OF CHANGES IN CREDIT CONDITIONS

Changes in interest rates and other credit conditions associated with countercyclical variations in the supply of money and credit influence economic developments through their effect on decisions to borrow and spend or to save and lend.

How Lenders and Savers Are Affected · Commercial banks' willingness to lend and the terms they offer are strongly influenced by monetary policy because it has a direct impact on their reserve positions. Other lenders, such as finance companies and mortgage companies, obtain part of their funds by borrowing from commercial banks. At times when credit expansion is under restraint, these lenders find that funds are less readily available and more expensive than in times of credit ease. As the volume of their borrowing is restricted and its cost rises, nonbank lenders may find it necessary to curtail their lending. They will also tend to charge customers higher rates of interest on loans. . . .

The flow of lendable funds in the over-all credit market depends to a large extent, however, on the saving of consumers, who make funds available to the market directly or through intermediary financial institutions. . . . How much total consumer saving will respond in given circumstances to changes in interest rates is a matter of some uncertainty. Nevertheless, changes in interest rates do have discernible effects on the distribution of the flow of consumer saving among various financial investments and also, to a degree, on the distribution of total consumer saving between financial investments and investments in capital goods.

How Business Borrowing and Spending Respond · The effect on borrowing and on spending of changes in credit conditions and costs will not be uniform among businesses and individuals. The effect will vary with—among other things—the reliance that is placed on credit by the potential borrowers, with the borrower's financial position and credit standing, and with his income and profit expectations.

In periods of restraint on the pace of monetary expansion, potential business borrowers will be discouraged in a number of ways. The pressure on banks to restrict the growth of their loan portfolios will lead them to ask some borowers to accept smaller loans and some to accept shorter maturities. In other instances banks may ask customers to postpone their borrowing altogether. And any rise in bank lending rates may also discourage some potential borrowers from seeking loans. Customers who want to borrow are likely to seek accommodation elsewhere, but these sources—nonbank financial institutions and the credit market generally—will also be under pressure as a result of the general excess of demand at current levels of interest rates.

The net effect of receding ease and eventual tightening of credit markets is likely to be some curtailment of spending by business. Forward inventory commitments, and later the actual purchases, may be curbed; and there may also be a slowing down in planned spending for plant and equipment.

These curtailments in spending may not affect the majority of businesses or the full amount of many loans, but they will affect some borrowers and the amounts involved in some loans. In other words, marginal borrowing will be restrained. The result usually is a smaller increase in spending than transactors would have wanted under more favorable credit conditions, rather than an actual contraction in spending. For this reason, the brake on business spending is difficult to observe.

The sensitivity of business spending and borrowing to changes in interest rates and other credit terms varies widely. The ability and willingness to accumulate inventories, for example, may be significantly affected for some enterprises by a rise in bank lending rates, while for others, whose inventory costs are smaller or whose financial position is stronger, such a rise may have little deterrent impact. In certain fields such as industrial and commercial construction, public utilities, and railroads, where there are large fixed investments, long-term interest rates are a particularly significant cost factor. In such fields comparatively small increases in interest rates can result in postponement of borrowing to finance capital outlays. Even in fields where interest costs incurred for financing fixed investment may be less important, as in retail and wholesale trade, some business units may be induced to cut back on their reliance on longer-term borrowing when interest rates rise, and other borrowers may be deterred from adding to such debt. . . .

Businesses borrow in the expectation that the return from the use of borowed funds will exceed interest costs by a significant margin. When the margin is large and when it is fairly well assured, moderate increases in interest rates may have little effect on the willingness of a business to borrow. But when the margin is smaller or when the return is less certain, a rise in interest rates discourages borrowers.

A rise in interest rates increases the cost of long-term borrowing and influences the utilization of productive resources through changes in the relationship between prices of existing capital assets and the cost of producing new assets. These changes direct some activity away from production of long-lived, slowly depreciating capital goods and thereby free resources for an immediate increase in output of consumer goods or of producers' equipment to make consumer goods. In the fixed-capital area these changes, together with changes in the outlook for profits and risks due to the altered credit and monetary situation, shift the balance of business decisions toward holding or buying old assets, and adapting such assets to new uses, as compared with producing new ones.

The relationship between capitalized values of existing assets and costs of producing new ones is indicated on the following page. The illustration pertains to an office building with a net income from rent of $100,000 a year.

If the current interest rate for such investment, with allowance for risk, were 6 percent, the capitalized value of the existing property would be more than the cost of constructing a new building with the same earning prospects. An investor in this type of real estate would build a new structure instead of buying an existing building, other things being equal.

Estimated cost of constructing a new building:	$1,500,000
Capitalized market value of an existing building with earnings from rent (net of all current costs and depreciation) of $100,000:	
If current interest rate, with allowance for risk, is 6 percent:	1,666,667
If current interest rate, with allowance for risk, is 7 percent:	1,428,571

On the other hand, if the relevant interest rate were 7 percent, it would not pay to build a new structure and the decision would go the other way. The economic resources that would have gone into constructing the new building would then be available for other uses.

How Consumer Borrowing and Spending Respond · Consumers make use of both short- and long-term credit. They use short- and intermediate-term credit to finance purchases of durable goods, home improvements, and a variety of services. Most of their long-term borowing takes the form of residential mortgages.

Various types of institutions extend short- and intermediate-term credit to consumers on fairly standardized terms and charge rates that are relatively inflexible and high in relation to open market rates of interest. The interest rate that a consumer-financing institution pays for the funds it borrows is only one of the cost elements in the finance charge to consumers, but it does have an influence on the institution's willingness to lend.

General credit tightness or ease will be transmitted to consumer credit through changes in the strictness or leniency of credit standards applied by institutions granting such credit. The variation of credit standards affects the volume of new credit extended, and this in turn affects the volume of consumer credit that is outstanding.

Even though the mortgage market is less highly organized than are markets for government and corporate obligations, and interest rates on mortgages are less sensitive to shifts in supply or demand pressures than are rates on other securities, the financing available for home purchases is considerably affected by credit conditions and interest rates.

Some lending institutions increase or decrease sharply the proportion of lendable funds they are willing to place in mortgages when interest rates on competing investment media fall or rise significantly. This tendency may be especially pronounced for Government-underwritten mortgages—FHA-insured or VA-guaranteed—because administrative ceilings on their contract rates make their actual market rates less flexible than those on other media.

As the availability of residential mortgage funds fluctuates, potential borrowers may encounter more or less difficulty in qualifying for mortgage loans. Borrowing to buy houses is typically long-term and repayable in monthly instalments. The ability of a potential borrower to qualify for a mortgage usually depends on the relationship of the monthly payment to his income. The standards that lenders apply in this respect depend in large measure on the availability of mortgage funds, and these standards become more stringent as the amount of funds available for lending declines.

In addition, any increase in interest rates on mortgages adds to the monthly payment. Thus marginal borrowers are no longer able to qualify on the basis of existing loan standards regarding the relation of the monthly mortgage payment to monthly income. In periods when over-all demand for goods and services is tending to be excessive, limitations on the pace of monetary expansion and on the availability of credit, together with increases in interest costs, tend to discourage house building or to encourage preferences for lower priced houses. In periods of economic slack and credit ease, increases in loanable funds and lower interest rates encourage residential construction. . . .

As the flows of spending, investing, and saving in the economy change in response to monetary policy and also to other circumstances, the reserve banking authorities are in a position to adapt current policies to these developments. If spending is tending to react too strongly or too weakly to policy shifts, the stance of policy can be altered. The gradualness with which policy has its effect, together with the inherent flexibility of monetary instruments, enables the reserve banking authorities to adapt to changing circumstances. At the same time, policy needs to be sensitive to, and also to anticipate, current economic tendencies and what they are likely to mean for the near-term future. Through these efforts the timing of policy is made consonant with the evolving course of the economy.

Monetary Policy and Economic Research

Harry G. Johnson, professor of economics at the University of Chicago, surveyed economists' thinking about monetary theory and policy in an article in the June 1962 issue of the American Economic Review.

THERE IS PROBABLY no field of economics in which the writings of economists are so strongly influenced by both current fashions in opinion and current problems of economic policy as the field of monetary policy.[1] In the period immediately after the war, economists writing on monetary policy were generally agreed that monetary expansion was of little use in combatting depression. Skepticism about the effectiveness of monetary restraint in combatting inflation was less marked, though some took the extreme view that monetary restraint would either prove ineffective or precipitate a collapse. But it was generally thought that the wartime legacy of a large and widely-held public debt was a major obstacle to the application of monetary restraint, both because it was feared that abandonment of the bond-support program adopted to assist war financing would destroy public confidence in government debt, and because the transfer from the government to the private banking system that would result from an increase in the interest payable on the latter's large holdings of public debt was regarded as undesirable. Economists therefore divided into those who advocated schemes for insulating bank-held government debt from general interest-rate movements, as a means of clearing the way for monetary restraint, and those who argued for an extension of selective credit controls.

The inflation that accompanied the Korean War forced the termination of the bond-support program, and thereafter monetary policy became the chief instrument for controlling short-run fluctuations. The nonmaterialization of the disastrous con-

1. The original text contains a detailed bibliography of recent writings in monetary economics, including references to the articles of the authors mentioned in this version.—*Editor.*

sequences that some had predicted would follow the termination of the bond-support program, together with the development of the availability doctrine (which enlisted liquidity preference on the side of monetary policy and made a widely-held public debt a help rather than a hindrance) strengthened confidence in the power of monetary restraint to control inflation, though the availability doctrine also provided ammunition to advocates of selective controls by depicting monetary policy as achieving its results through irrational and discriminatory mechanisms. Subsequent experience, together with empirical and theoretical research, has fairly conclusively disposed of the availability doctrine's most appealing feature—the proposition that the central bank can produce large reductions in private spending by means of small increases in interest rates—and research has tended to refute the contention that monetary policy operates discriminatorily. Nevertheless, the availability doctrine has left its mark on the field, inasmuch as the majority of monetary economists would probably explain how monetary policy influences the economy by reference to its effects on the availability and cost of credit, with the stress on availability.

Trust in the power of monetary restraint to control inflation has been further reduced by the coexistence of rising prices and higher average unemployment in the late 1950's, and the associated revival and elaboration of cost-push theories of inflation. On the other hand, experience of monetary policy in three mild business cycles has revived confidence in the efficacy of monetary expansion in combatting recessions and dispelled the belief that monetary restraint in a boom will do either nothing or far too much. In fact, the wheel has come full circle, and prevailing opinion has returned to the characteristic 1920's view that monetary policy is probably more effective in checking deflation than in checking inflation.

Changing fashions in prevailing opinion apart, the revival of monetary policy as a major branch of economic policy has stimulated much controversy, thought, and research on all aspects of monetary policy. In addition, the legacy of war debt and the increased size and frequency of government debt operations that it has entailed, together with the difficulties created for the Treasury by "bills only" and other Federal Reserve and governmental policies, has brought the whole subject of debt management within the purview of monetary economists as a special form of open-market operations. . . .

THE OBJECTIVES AND INSTRUMENTAL ROLE OF MONETARY POLICY

In pre-Keynesian days, monetary policy was the single established instrument of aggregative economic policy, and price stability was its established objective. The Keynesian revolution introduced an alternative instrument, fiscal policy, and a second objective, maintenance of full employment (now more commonly described as economic stability), which might conflict with the objective of price stability. Since the war, debt management has been added almost universally to the list of instruments; and since the middle 1950's many economists have added a third item—adequately rapid economic growth—to the list of objectives. In recent years the balance-of-payments problem has been forcing the admission of a fourth objective—international balance —and may eventually establish a fourth instrument—foreign economic policy.

Recognition of several objectives of economic policy introduces the possibility of a conflict of objectives requiring resolution by a compromise. This possibility and its implications have been more clearly recognized elsewhere than in the United States, where there has been a tendency to evade the issue by denying the possibility of conflict or by insisting that conflicts be eliminated by some other means than sacrifice of the achievement of any of the objectives. Where a conflict of objectives has been clearly recognized—notably in the criticisms directed at the anti-inflationary emphasis of Federal Reserve policy in 1957–60— the arguments about alternative compromises have been qualitative and nonrigorous: rigorous theoretical exploration and quantitative assessment of the costs and benefits of alternative compromises between conflicting policy objectives remain to be undertaken.

The availability of alternative policy instruments introduces the question of their absolute and comparative effectiveness; research on this range of problems has been undertaken by a number of economists, but has not progressed far towards an accepted body of knowledge. As already mentioned, monetary policy since 1951 has resumed a large part of the responsibility for short-run economic stabilization—a consequence of both the inadaptability of the budgetary process to the requirements of a flexible fiscal policy and the domination of the budget by other objectives of national policy than stabilization. Reliance on monetary policy for this purpose has raised the question of how effectively the task is likely to be performed. The argument for using monetary policy is usually expressed in terms of the "flexibility" of monetary policy, by which is often meant no more than that monetary policy can be changed quickly. But the real issues are whether the monetary authorities are likely to take appropriate action at the right time, and whether the effects of monetary action on the economy occur soon enough and reliably enough to have a significant stabilizing effect.

As to the first question, there is general agreement that the Federal Reserve has committed errors in the timing, extent and duration of policy changes. Most economists seem inclined to trust the System to improve its performance with experience and the benefit of their criticism. Some, however, are so distrustful of discretionary authority in principle, or so skeptical of the feasibility of effective stabilization by monetary means, as to advocate that the Federal Reserve should not attempt short-run stabilization, but should confine itself (or be confined) to expanding the money supply at a steady rate appropriate to the growth of the economy. The proposal to substitute a monetary rule for the discretion of the monetary authority is not of course new— Henry Simons' classic statement of the case for it appeared in the 1930's—but the definition of the rule in terms of the rate of monetary expansion rather than stability of a price index reflects both the modern concern with growth and a more sophisticated understanding of the stabilization problem.

Whether such a rule would have produced better results than the policy actually followed in the past is a difficult matter to test. Milton Friedman has discussed the difficulties and some abortive tests that tend to favor a 4 percent annual increase rule. Martin Bronfenbrenner has devised a more elaborate series of tests of alternative rules, including discretionary policy; his results for annual data 1901–1958 (excluding the Second World War) show that a 3 percent annual increase rule comes closest to the "ideal pattern" defined by price stability, though his subsequent tests on quarterly data from 1947 on suggest the superiority of a "lag rule" relating changes in the money supply to prior changes in the labor force, productivity and velocity. These tests are subject to statistical and theoretical objections, but they open up an interesting new line of research. In the absence of a definitely specified standard of comparison, discussions of the appropriateness of the central bank's monetary policy tend to fall back on textual criticism of its explanation of its actions or the exercise of personal judgment about what policy should have been.

The question of the extent of the stabilizing effect that monetary action may be expected to achieve was first raised, at the formal theoretical level, by Friedman, who argued that policies intended to stabilize the economy might well have destabilizing effects because of the lags involved in their operation. Subsequent work and discussion on this aspect of monetary policy has concentrated on the length and variability of the lag in the effect of monetary policy. . . . Thomas Mayer estimates the lag in the reaction of investment expenditure and consumer credit outstanding to monetary policy changes, sector by sector, and taking into account lags in monetary-policy changes and the multiplier process, concludes that monetary policy operates on the economy much too slowly for its effects to be quickly reversed; from a computation of the effect that an optimally-timed monetary policy would have had on the stability of industrial production over six business cycles, he concludes that monetary policy is too inflexible to reduce the fluctuation of industrial production by more than about 5 to 10 percent on the average. W. H. White has since argued that Mayer seriously overestimates the average lag, and that the correct estimate would provide almost ideal conditions for effective anticyclical policy; White also remarks that Mayer's results do not show the destabilizing effects indicated as possible by Friedman's analysis.

Friedman's contention that monetary policy operates with a long and variable lag figures largely in his opposition to discretionary monetary policy. . . . Friedman has produced a lengthy defense of his measure of the lag, together with other supporting evidence. This defense indicates that the measurement of the lag raises much more subtle and fundamental theoretical and methodological issues than appear at first sight.

A study of lags in fiscal and monetary policy by Brown, Solow, Ando and Kareken attempts to estimate the lag between the indication of a need for a change in monetary policy and the effect of the resulting change in policy on output, and finds that a substantial stabilizing effect is achieved within six to nine months. They also find that fiscal policy operating on disposable income is a more powerful stabilizer, achieving as much as half of its effect within six months.

This research on the lag in effect of monetary policy has been orientated towards determining the efficacy of monetary policy as a stabilizer, on the assumption that monetary policy is decided with reference to contemporaneous economic conditions. Little if any research has been devoted to the more ambitious task of designing optimal systems of changing monetary policy in response to movements of relevant economic indicators. A. W. Phillips and, more recently, W. J. Baumol have shown that what seem like sensible procedures for changing a policy variable in response to changing conditions may well aggravate instability. . . .

THE EFFECTIVENESS OF MONETARY POLICY

To turn from the instrumental role of monetary policy to the related but broader questions of how monetary action influences the economy, and how effectively, the prevailing tendency has been to approach these questions by analyzing how monetary policy, and particularly open-market operations, affect the spending decisions of particular sectors of the economy. This formulation of the problem is a natural corollary of Keynesian theory, and the evolution of the analysis since the war has closely reflected the evolution of monetary theory, though with a perceptible lag; but the analysis has also been strongly influenced by the availability doctrine. That doctrine, the formulation of which was largely the work of Robert Roosa emerged in the later years of the bond-support program as a solution to the conflict between the belief that a large widely-held public debt obliged the central bank to confine interest-rate movements to narrow limits and the belief that large interest-rate changes were necessary to obtain significant effects on spending.

The doctrine comprised two central propositions. The first was that widespread holding of public debt, particularly by financial institutions and corporations, facilitates monetary control by transmitting the influence of interest-rate changes effected by open-market operations through the economy. The second was that small interest-rate changes could, by generating or dispelling uncertainty about future rates and by inflicting or eliminating capital losses that institutions were unwilling to realize by actual sales ("the pinning-in effect"), achieve significant effects on spending even if the demands of spenders for credit were interest-inelastic—these effects being achieved by influencing the willingness of lenders to lend or, put another way, by influencing the availability of credit to borrowers by altering the terms of credit and the degree of credit rationing. The second proposition has turned out on subsequent investigation to depend on incorrect empirical assumptions about institutional behavior, particularly with respect to "the pinning-in effect," and on a doubtful asymmetry between the reactions of lender and borrower expectations to interest-rate changes, as well as to involve some logical inconsistencies. Nevertheless, the doctrine and discussion of it have helped to popularize the concept of "availability of credit" as one of the main variables on which monetary policy operates.

"Availability" actually comprises a number of disparate elements—the liquidity of potential lenders' and spenders' assets, the terms on which lenders will extend or borrowers can obtain credit, and the degree to which credit is rationed among eligible borrowers. Emphasis on these factors as influences on spending has provided new arguments for those who favor selective credit controls—specific arguments for controls where the terms of credit rather than the cost of credit seem the effective determinant of spending decisions, as in the case of instalment credit, and a general defensive argument based on the discriminatory character of credit rationing. The most powerful attack on the discriminatory character of allegedly general methods of economic control has come from J. K. Galbraith, who has maintained that the use of monetary and fiscal policy has favored the monopolistic at the expense of the competitive sectors of the economy to an extent comparable to repeal of the antitrust laws. Others have maintained that monetary restraint discriminates against small business. Empirical studies by Bach and Huizenga and Allen Meltzer show that this is not true of bank credit; Meltzer's study finds that while small firms have greater difficulty in obtaining nonbank credit in tight periods than large firms, this discrimination tends to be offset by extension of trade credit from large firms to small.

The emphasis on the availability of credit as a determinant of expenditure has led to a critical re-examination of the business-attitude survey findings that formerly were used as evidence that business investment is insensitive to monetary policy. In addition, monetary theorists have tended to raise their estimates of the sensitivity of business investment to changes in the cost of credit. These reassessments have been based on the opinion that investors' expected profits are more finely and rationally calculated than used to be thought, rather than on any impressive new empirical evidence of such sensitivity. The most definite new empirical evidence there is confirms the long time theoretically established sensitivity of residential construction to interest-rate changes, and even this sensitivity has been attributed in part to the influence of ceiling rates on federally-guaranteed mortgages on the willingness of institutional lenders to lend on such mortgages. The failure of empirical research to disclose such sensitivity may be the consequence of too simple a theoretical approach, the attempt to relate a flow of expenditure on assets to the cost of credit without adequate recognition of the range of alternative assets or the complexities of stock-adjustment processes. The new approach to monetary dynamics described in the previous part suggests that a more sophisticated theory of real investment is necessary for successful empirical work; on the other hand, some empirical works suggests that better results might be achieved by working with changes in the quantity of money than by attempting to determine the influence of changes in interest rates on particular categories of spending.

The discussion of the effectiveness of monetary policy just described has been concerned with monetary policy operating in a given institutional environment. Since the middle 1950's a new debate has been opened up, concerned with the fact that traditional methods of monetary control are primarily directed at commercial bank credit, and the possibility that institutional change stimulated by monetary restriction may reduce the effectiveness of traditional techniques of monetary control. The main debate has been concerned with Gurley and Shaw's contention that the growth of financial intermediaries, prompted in part by the competitive handicaps imposed on commercial banks for purposes of monetary control, progressively provides close substitutes for money the presence of which weakens the grip of monetary policy on the economy; and with their suggestion that the controlling powers of the central bank should be extended beyond the commercial banks to other financial institutions. . . . From the point of view of monetary policy, the central issue is . . . whether the liabilities of financial intermediaries are such close substitutes for money that monetary restriction is substantially offset through substitution for bank deposits of other financial claims backed by only a small fractional reserve of money—in short, whether financial intermediaries substantially increase the interest-elasticity of demand for money. This is an empirical question; and the empirical evidence so far is that shifts by the public from money into thrift assets in periods of monetary restraint have not had a significant influence on velocity.

The Postwar Record of Monetary Policy

HENRY C. WALLICH and
STEPHEN H. AXILROD

This review and appraisal of Federal Reserve actions in the post-war era was written for the 1964 edition of the American Assembly's volume U.S. Monetary Policy. Professor Wallich's co-author, Stephen H. Axilrod, is the chief of the Government Finance Section at the Board of Governors of the Federal Reserve System.

IN THE NATURE OF things, a definitive appraisal is possible, if at all, only of matters dead and gone. Monetary policy today is very much alive. All that this chapter can hope to offer, consequently, is an interim report. . . .

FROM THE END OF THE WAR TO THE ACCORD OF 1951

At the end of World War II, the fortunes of Federal Reserve policy had reached their all-time low. They had been declining ever since the fateful days in 1929 and 1930, when the weight of monetary policy, at least as it was then conceived by policy-makers, had been thrown against the onrushing depression—but to no visible effect. They had continued to drop throughout the 1930's as other agencies of the federal government expanded their monetary, fiscal, and political powers—although the possibility that the Federal Reserve did not do as much as it might have cannot be denied. The nadir was reached in 1945 when the Treasury, having availed itself of the Federal Reserve for war financing, expected the System to remain a continuing and submissive instrument for solving the problems of federal debt management.

Struggle to Free Monetary Policy · With a federal debt of over $250 billion, a new phenomenon fraught, it was thought at war's end, with unforeseeable consequences, the System's chief function had become stabilization of the government securities market. The pattern of interest rates had to be preserbed by appropriate purchases and sales; the Treasury's refunding operations had to be supported; in general, the market had to be watched continually and treated with the utmost circumspection, for it was thought that any attempts to raise interest rates, except perhaps on the shortest maturities, would intensify the danger of panicky market movements that might upset the economy. It must be remembered that at that time many analysts feared a postwar depression. . . .

At this low point in its fortunes the System made two basic decisions. First, it rejected the view that depression was the country's main danger and, instead, geared its expectations to inflation; and second, it clung to the principle of general credit control as the core of monetary policy.

In its struggle to make this principle prevail, the System's chief antagonist was, of course, the United States Treasury Department. In the immediate postwar years both became concerned about inflation, but the Treasury took the view that to try to control inflation by raising interest rates was useless at best and dangerous at worst. Given the huge debt and an overexpanded money supply, both inherited from the war, nothing could be achieved, short of massive measures, by trying to influence the liquidity of the public. On the other hand, massive measures might bring about a collapse of the bond market, the public credit, and perhaps the entire economy. . . .

Beginnings of a Flexible Policy · In the second half of 1947, the Treasury at long last agreed to let the Federal Reserve withdraw support from Treasury bills and certificates, the chief short-term instruments. This created the first modest amount of "elbowroom" for monetary policy. But the necessity of keeping the long rate from rising above an agreed-upon level meant that monetary policy could operate flexibly only within very narrow limits. If attempts at monetary restraint or growth in credit demands forced commercial bank and, in general, market sales of long-term securities, the Federal Reserve was compelled to buy them, thus supplying reserves to banks to keep the rate from rising above the ceiling; since rate pressures were for the most part upward, the ceiling was in effect a peg of the long rate.

The revival of strong inflationary pressures at the time of the Korean outbreak in 1950 raised, in a very pointed way, the question of Federal Reserve independence to pursue a counter cyclical and, when required, an anti-inflationary monetary policy. At the same time, the Treasury was faced with the possibility of new large-scale federal financing, which would be facilitated by continued Federal Reserve market-support policies.

The ensuing and at times severe conflict was terminated by the Accord of March 4, 1951. The two agencies agreed that the government bond market was to find its own level subject to a number of actions designed to smooth the transition and ease the Treasury's financing problems. In effect, the peg was removed gradually, and the Federal Reserve became free to conduct open-market operations for counter cyclical purposes. Monetary policy at last had regained its freedom.

An Appraisal of Pre-Accord Policies · It may be true, but not quite fair, to say that monetary policy in the pre-Accord period accomplished a good deal less than it might have. Experience since the Accord indicates that the market risks inherent in tightening credit and letting the bond market find its own level may have been greatly exaggerated at the time. But given the undigested nature of the federal debt, much of it loosely held, the danger was, and still is, difficult to assess.

Assuming the danger was exaggerated—a tall assumption from the Treasury's point of view—how much of the postwar inflation might have been avoided by timely monetary restraints? Any answer is in large part guesswork. But bearing in mind the delayed impact of inflation suppressed by wartime controls, the increases in labor and materials costs that had occurred, the shortage of supplies, the exceptionally large overhanging liquidity of consumers and of many firms, one probably does not go wrong in thinking that monetary restraint, however skillfully applied, would have had a limited effect at best. The major part of the postwar inflation was probably unavoidable.

POST-ACCORD POLICIES

The Treasury-Federal Reserve Accord opened a new era for United States monetary policy. It allowed monetary policy to be guided by criteria of economic growth and stability, unfettered by considerations of debt management. It thereby provided for freely fluctuating short- and long-term interest rates, subject to certain Federal Reserve commitments designed to help Treasury financing, to smooth the transition to the new regime, and to contain disorderly market conditions. . . .

The period from the spring of 1951 to the end of 1963 provided the Federal Reserve with an interesting, not to say puzzling, assortment of situations. Three broad subperiods can be distinguished: one, roughly 1951–58, when economic cycles occurred against a background of high employment and at times creeping inflation; a second, 1958–60, which can be termed a watershed, in which old problems were abating and new ones were coming forward; and a third, 1960–63, in which the new problems of persistent balance-of-payments deficit, excessive unemployment, and (at least in the eyes of some observers) lagging economic growth required revision of older views about how policy should operate.

High Employment and Creeping Inflation, 1951–58 · The first post-Accord period of high activity combined with monetary restraint ended in the summer of 1953. It might be argued that the timing of the turn was influenced by a sudden tightening of the market induced perhaps by overly hasty tightening actions— and, more particularly, intimations of tightening to come—by the Federal Reserve and the Treasury in the spring of 1953. But one would have to assign very great power to monetary effects to believe that the 1953 downturn was brought on in any significant degree through market reactions that raised interest rates—by what in terms of later experience seems a moderate amount—in anticipation, perhaps partly misguided, that a real monetary squeeze was ahead.

The 1953–54 downturn was characterized chiefly by its mildness; this, in fact, has been a characteristic of all the postwar recessions. In that period the Federal Reserve moved quickly and decisively. System actions to ease credit conditions through open-market purchases of securities and a cut in reserve requirements helped bring down rates on Treasury bills from 2.30 percent to as low as 0.60 percent in the spring of 1954 and on long-term government bonds from 3¼ percent to 2½ percent. Stimulative actions also led to rapid expansion of commercial banks' loans and investments, mainly the latter, and of bank deposits, mainly time deposits.

The System's actions were powerfully assisted at that time by a tax cut. Aided by the underlying strength of demand, these measures helped to turn the cycle upwards in the second half of

1954. The apparent success of fiscal and monetary policies may not have been without some costs, however. The increase in bank liquidity as a result of stimulative Federal Reserve policies immunized the banks to some extent against subsequent pressure. The difficulties the System encountered in exerting restraint in the next expansion are traceable in some measure to the liquidity reserves that it had supplied banks with during the 1954 period of ease.

There were, however, strong enough inflationary forces at work in the expansion of 1955–57 and in the circumstances of the time —featuring the exuberant capital-spending boom and upward-cost pressures—so that it would have been difficult at best for the System to contain inflation more successfully than it did. Prices rose most of the time—wholesale prices from mid-1955 and consumer prices from early 1956. The steadiness of the rise through 1957 brought the term "creeping inflation" into popular use and made many wonder if inflationary psychology had become an important influence on economic decision-making in the private economy. Stock prices, which had risen sharply in 1954, continued to rise substantially in 1955 and early 1956; and real estate values again began rising after a post-Korean period of stability.

The end of the cyclical expansion and boom that began around mid-1954 came in the summer of 1957, as indicated by the behavior of gross national product in real terms. The rise in production had become quite moderate by 1956 and 1957, however, but price rises persisted. The Federal Reserve had steadily tightened money in the expansionary period in order to contain inflationary pressures. The timing of the last tightening action in this period— raising the discount rate by a ½ percentage point to 3½ percent in the late summer of 1957—turned out to be unfortunate, for it came virtually at the top of the boom and onset of recession.

Along with the progressive tightening of money and credit, the timing of the discount-rate action made it easier to argue that Federal Reserve policy contributed significantly to the end of the boom. But the appearance of excess capacity provides a more plausible explanation of the downturn. The surge in business capital spending and a large rise in inventory accumulation seem to have created imbalances between areas of heavy business investment—such as autos and steel—and the emerging pattern of consumer expenditures.

The 1957–58 downturn was brief but sharp. Between the summer of 1957 and winter of 1958, which was the cyclical low, gross national product in real terms fell by about 9 percent (annual rate). In efforts to reverse the decline, the Federal Reserve took actions to ease credit conditions. The discount rate was reduced by ½ point in the fall of 1957 and subsequent reductions were made in rapid order in early 1958. Member banks found themselves with enough reserve funds to reduce their indebtedness to Federal Reserve Banks and to restore in some degree their reduced liquidity. As reserve positions continued to be eased through open-market operations and reserve-requirement reductions, bank credit became readily available, and money supply, after declining in the latter part of 1957, rose rather rapidly in 1958, as did time deposits at commercial banks.

In this atmosphere of active ease, market participants, who had more and more become aware of the flexible interest rate implications of anticyclical monetary policy, discounted a good part of the expected market effect of the policy of monetary ease. Demand for U.S. government securities in anticipation of still higher security prices was so strong that short-term rates dropped precipitately from about 3½ percent to under 1 percent and bond yields dropped from around 3¾ percent to 3¼ percent. . . .

The Watershed, 1958–60 · The cyclical upswing that began in 1958 was comparatively brief—lasting but two years—and was associated with the emergence of developments that were to persist, as it turned out, into the early 1960s, and which were to distinguish the years 1958–63 sharply from the 1951–58 period. Gradually, both policy objectives and operating techniques were adapted to the new set of problems.

One characteristic of the 1958–60 upswing was that it stopped short of satisfactory levels of employment. The unemployment rate, which had averaged a little more than 4 percent in the years 1955–57, averaged 5.5 percent in 1959 and just about 5 percent over the first five months of 1960, when the upswing was phasing out.

Another emerging characteristic of the economy in the years 1958–60 was comparative stability in the average level of prices. Consumer prices rose, but at a slower pace than in the earlier upswing. Wholesale prices, meanwhile, stabilized on average. These price developments in part stemmed from the incompleteness of recovery from the previous recession, which was reflected in idle plant capacity and manpower resources. In turn, the price developments, as they continued, tended to modify the inflationary expectations that had been generated by previous price advances.

The third characteristic of this watershed period was the enlargement of the United States balance-of-payments deficit with other countries. The United States had been running a deficit for most of the postwar period but it was moderate in size and served the useful purpose of enabling foreign countries to build up their war-depleted liquidity reserves by adding to dollar holdings. There was little drain on the U.S. gold stock associated with the moderate deficits because foreign countries placed most of their new net dollar funds in deposits with U.S. banks or in the U.S. government securities. But in 1958 and 1959 the deficit was substantially enlarged (from an annual average of less than $1 billion in 1951–57 to $3.6 billion in 1958–59) as our export surplus narrowed; and foreign countries, already well supplied with dollars, took a substantial portion of their net earnings in gold. In the two years 1958 and 1959, our gold stock declined by $3.3 billion to a level of $19.5 billion, whereas it had declined only about half that much in the eight years from the end of 1949, when the gold stock was close to its postwar peak of $24.7 billion, to the end of 1957.

Monetary policy was indeed tightened rather more than domestic economic conditions seemed to warrant in the latter part of 1958 and in 1959, but this seemed to have been less a response to the emerging balance-of-payments situation than it was to the experience of 1954–55, when massive easing and slowness to tighten had made it difficult for the Federal Reserve to regain control of bank credit later on. In addition, there appeared to be lingering inflationary fears. . . .

While monetary policy may have been too tight in 1959, the Federal Reserve in early 1960 apparently did anticipate the need to combat a possible recession—or, at a minimum, the System saw that inflationary conditions were waning. This was brought home to the Federal Reserve by the sharp decline in interest rates in the early months of 1960, in response to the bearish market expectations that emerged when it became apparent that the economy was not so buoyant as many expected it would be and when it also became clear that the federal government was going to run a budgetary surplus in 1960. While money supply declined from mid-1959 to about mid-1960, banks in the first half of 1960 were able to reduce borrowings from the Federal Reserve to quite low levels. At the onset of the 1960 recession, conditions were favorable to rapid monetary expansion, in contrast with the situation at the onset of recession in 1957, when banks were still heavily in debt.

Many would argue, however, that open-market operations should have been more stimulative in early 1960, and the discount rate should have been reduced earlier than it was. The Federal Reserve discount rate, which had been raised gradually from a low of 1¾ percent in the spring of 1958 to a high of 4 percent in the late summer of 1959, was not reduced until June, 1960 (then by half a point), and was reduced again in August to a level of 3 percent. More stimulative policies, it is said, would have kept the money supply from declining in the early part of 1960 and thereby kept the economy from going into recession. Whether money alone would have had so powerful an effect is, of course, conjectural. In addition, there was the risk of very heavy outflows of capital abroad from the even greater declines in interest rates that would likely have been the product of a more expansionary open-market policy at that time. In fact, a sharp rise in capital outflows abroad was a major problem in 1960, even though the yield on three-month Treasury bills did not fall below the 2.10 percent to 2.40 percent range, and led to increasing concern with the balance of payments by the monetary authorities.

The Domestic Economy and the Balance of Payments, 1960–63 · The recession that began in the late spring of 1960 was over by the winter of 1961, by which time gross national product in real terms had fallen by only 2.5 percent at an annual rate. From the winter of 1961 through 1963 real gross national product rose steadily, although at times hesitatingly. Nevertheless, there was considerable dissatisfaction with the performance of the domestic economy because unemployment did not go below 5.5 percent of the labor force in almost three years of expansion. . . .

Increased capital outflows from this country to major financial centers abroad played an important role in continuance of the balance-of-payments deficit in 1960 and for several years after. This increased the concern of the monetary authorities with the balance of payments since a good part of the capital flowed abroad as a result of the policy of monetary ease being pursued in this country to encourage domestic economic expansion. With domestic money market conditions easy, funds flowed abroad because higher interest returns were available there or because borrowers took advantage of the ready availability of credit here. For instance, in 1960 and 1961 short-term capital outflows from this country were $1.3 billion and $1.5 billion, respectively, mostly representing bank loans to foreigners, after averaging less than $300 million a year in the previous seven years. . . .

The juxtaposition of a balance-of-payments problem, as intensified by rather heavy capital outflows, and a problem of domestic unemployment led to several adaptations in the operations of monetary policy. Basically, these all represented efforts to encourage domestic credit expansion without at the same time putting much downward pressure on short-term interest rates.

Faced with the need to minimize downward pressure on short-term rates, the Federal Reserve in the period of recession and recovery did not reduce the discount rate below the 3 percent to which it had been lowered in the summer of 1960. Thus, it was not lowered by as much as in earlier recessions. In the fall of 1962, reserves were released to banks through a reduction in the reserve requirement against time deposits in the hope that this would provide reserves to banks with a minimum downward effect on short-term rates, for reserves would otherwise have had to be supplied, it was argued, through open-market purchases of mainly short-term securities. The Federal Reserve after the Accord had often reduced requirements, but usually in recessions, to provide reserves immediately to all parts of the country.

Abandonment of "Bills Only" · The principal adaptation in monetary instruments to cope with the short-term interest rate problem during the 1960–63 period was the abandonment in early 1961 of the "bills only" policy that had been followed since 1953. By late 1960 it had become apparent that open-market operations would have to be extended into the longer-term area if downward pressures were to be taken off short-term interest rates for balance-of-payments purposes while bank credit expansion was being promoted to encourage domestic economic growth. With open-market operations the most steadily used instrument of policy bacause of its inherent flexibility, an expansion in its operating scope would enable reserves to be provided through purchases of longer-term securities, which would relieve short rates of the immediate pressures associated with open-market purchases of Treasury bills. Of course, when commercial banks bought short-term securities in the process of using the reserves made available to them, such rates would tend to decline. However, this could be offset, at least in part, by Federal Reserve sales of Treasury bills, which would add to the market supply available for bank purchase. Such operations were in fact undertaken. . . .

The policy of buying long and selling short came to be known popularly as "operation twist" because it represented an effort to move short and long rates in different directions by official actions —to get short rates up and long rates down—in opposition to historical market tendencies for such rates to generally move in the same direction, although with different amplitude and speed of movement. The Federal Reserve itself never officially admitted to a sustained effort to reduce long rates, although it was certainly clear to all concerned that this was a worthwhile by-product of efforts to minimize downward, or exert upward, pressure on short rates. . . .

An Appraisal of Policy Caught between Two Fires · Many have argued that the Federal Reserve in the 1960–63 period did not do all it could to expand the domestic economy. Others have said that the balance of payments was not attacked vigorously enough. What can we say about the two issues—recognizing that, as of this writing, the fires are still burning, though it is not clear how hotly? . . .

While certainty about the exact degree is lacking, it does seem that both domestic spending and international capital flows are responsive to interest rates and associated credit availabilities. Domestic investments in homes and plant and equipment, for instance, are generally considered to be influenced to some extent by long-term interest rates. On the international side, we can feel sure that short-term capital flows between the United States and foreign financial centers are responsive to differentials in short-term interest rates and credit availabilities, although we cannot be sure by how much or to what extent other conditions (such as confidence, or lack of same, in the currency) may be offsetting or contributory, Long-term capital outflows too are responsive to differentials in credit conditions, and, like short-term flows, were a source of balance-of-payments troubles in the early 1960s. To moderate long-term outflows, an interest-equalization tax on foreign long-term securities was proposed by the Kennedy Administration in 1963. This tax, which would in effect add to the interest cost of such securities, was thought a mode desirable alternative either to direct capital controls or to an even tighter monetary policy that might have imperiled domestic investment.

In evaluating the impact of changes in interest rates and credit conditions on the domestic economy and the balance of payments, the majority o fthe Federal Open Market Committee apparently felt that the truth—or at least virtue, as Aristotle would have it—lay somewhere in between the extremes, and that neither the possible beneficial effects of rising interest rates on the balance of payments nor their possible damaging effects on the domestic economy could be ignored. Given the balance-of-payments problem, and the contributory role of short- and long-term capital outflows (including bank loans to foreigners) in the deficit, it seems clear that the Federal Reserve felt constrained in what it could do to expand bank credit and money domestically. . . .

While monetary policy performed pretty well (as evidenced by the continued expansion of money supply and bank credit and by the comparatively limited rises in interest rates) in a difficult situation, it was not by any means an unqualified success. In the final analysis, though, and in view of our continuing international and domestic economic problems in the period, monetary policy may well have been asked to do too much. Fiscal policy, while it was expansive, was not expansive enough. Hindsight makes it clear that a tax cut early in the period—say 1961 or 1962—might have helped the domestic economy and freed monetary policy to make a more concerted attack on the balance of payments.

Judgments about monetary policy in this period can at best be tentative, though, because at the present moment we are still in the midst of a very long period of cyclical upswing. Yet it is clear that Federal Reserve authorities showed flexibility and a degree of ingenuity in dealing with problems generated by the juxtaposition of large balance-of-payments deficits and a recalcitrant economy. Even so, the experience of the early 1960s—not to mention experience with other problems in earlier years—demonstrated the need for an even more coordinated use of all public policy instruments than was actually achieved.

The Case for an Automatic Monetary Pilot
EDWARD S. SHAW

Edward S. Shaw advanced his proposal for built-in growth of the money supply in a paper presented to the American Assembly in 1958. The author is professor of economics at Stanford University.

THERE ARE NUMEROUS alternative designs for a monetary system. The design that this country has hit upon builds into the monetary system an enormous capacity for both inflation and deflation. In successive trips back to the Congressional fix-it shop, the system's elasticity has been increased. As it is now put together, the United States monetary system is a brilliant solution for short-period instability in some security markets. But it has financed long-period inflation on the commodity markets, interrupted by painful episodes of excessive deceleration in monetary growth and declines in price levels. In its first half-century, the system has not created the temperate monetary environment that is most congenial to stable growth in real terms.

Now that the monetary system is undergoing revaluation, fundamental changes in its design should at least be discussed. The writer's own feeling is that, on balance, there would be improvement in its performance if the monetary system were put on automatic pilot. This suggestion is not a new one. The Reserve Board had to contend thirty years ago with proposals for automatized monetary control and turned them down in favor of "judgment in matters of credit administration."

What instructions are to be fed into an automatic monetary pilot? From the long list of alternatives that have been proposed in the history of monetary thought, one of the simplest appears most feasible. It is that, year in and year out, the nominal supply of money should increase by the *average* rate of growth in demand for nominal money at a stable level of commodity prices. According to usual estimates, which should be refined, the appropriate annual growth rate would be on the order of 3–4 percent.

For any good other than money, no eyebrows would rise over the premise that it is right to balance supply with demand. But "demand for money" is not a concept in popular use. There is no mention of it in the Federal Reserve Act. Only one small tabulation remotely akin to it is published in the *Federal Reserve Bulletin*. If the demand for money is to be considered as the standard for regulation of money supply, a moment spent in probing demand may not be amiss.

THE "DEMAND STANDARD" FOR MONETARY CONTROL

The pure gold standard is an automatic rule of monetary control. And so is pure bimetallism. The automatic rule that I am reviving for consideration may be termed the "demand standard" of monetary control. What it means can be worked out very simply with the help of a familiar expression:

$$MV = PT$$

The Money Equation · All symbol-scarred veterans of elementary economics will recall that M is the average nominal supply of money during a period of time. V stands for the average frequency in turnover for a unit of money against the flow of goods and services from the community's productive facilities. P is the price level of goods and services, and T is their physical quantity —the national real income.

The money equation is a better tool for our use if it is twisted a little:

$$M = (1/V) \ (P) \ (T)$$

A second twist replaces the inconvenient expression $1/V$ with k and changes the order of terms:

$$M = P(kT)$$

Now we have the nominal supply of money M counterpoised against the community's demand for nominal money $P(kT)$. The community's demand for money in real measure—for money balances in terms of their purchasing power is kT alone. And k is simply a proportion, a desired proportion, between the community's real balances in money and the community's real income. With its seasonal and cyclical wrinkles ironed out, k is a remarkably stable relationship. In this country, k increased through the nineteenth century and apparently changed very little after 1900 in trend measurements. For present purposes, it may be stipulated that real money is a commodity, demand for which now grows at the same rate as real national income. Demand for money, of course, is motivated both by the utility of money as a means of payment and by the safety of money as a fixed price asset.

Equality between M and $P(kT)$ is probably rare and fleeting. When it happens, there is monetary equilibrium. At all other times there is monetary disequilibrium. During most of the Treasury's tenure in monetary control, disequilibrium has been in the inflationary direction. Then M has exceeded $P(kT)$ at a stable level of prices P, so that money has been in excess supply. During approximately one-half of the Board's tenure, disequilibrium has been in the deflationary direction. Then M has been depressed below $P(kT)$ at a stable level of prices, so that money has been in excess demand.

Under the Demand Standard of monetary control, the automatic pilot would be instructed to increase M in step with the long-run growth rate of T. On the evidence that k is disposed to stability and on the judgment that a constant P is optimal for our economy and our social structure, the automatic pilot would link growth in money to growth in output of goods and services. Better evidence may turn up that k rises a little as we produce more goods *per capita*, and the view may win out that a little price inflation is good for us. Then the automatic pilot would be instructed to be a little more generous with the supply of nominal money. In effect, the pilot would be told to aim for the spot where monetary equilibrium should be, and not to worry about missing its target in the short run.

Missing the Turns in Monetary Control · Responsibility for monetary control other than by a fixed and simple rule, is too heavy a cross to thrust upon Treasury officials or upon a small group of men in an independent agency. A quick glance over possible disturbances to monetary equilibrium may indicate why some monetary technicians do conclude that automation is overdue in monetary control.

Economic systems must grow—in effective labor force, in productive capital, in output T. According to the money equation, growth in output increases demand for money. Other things equal, it creates excess demand for money. But other things do not long remain equal. If the community has less money than it wants, it reduces demand for goods. Then growth in output implies unwanted growth in inventories. Inventories full to overflowing may be cleared by price reductions, but prices reduced in an unbalanced way cannot be relied upon to dispel excess supply of goods and excess demand for money. Price deflation is painful, and it can cumulate out of all proportion to its initial cause.

Excess demand for money is not cured by economy in demand for money k. Instead k may rise, as deflation threatens, and accentuate excess demand for money. The sensible solution for a shortage in money balances is simply creation of more money balances, in nominal amount, by the monetary system.

Consider a second source of monetary instability. The k in the money equation is stable in longer periods, not seasonally and not cyclically. Business recession is initiated by an increase in k that precedes the cyclical turning point apparently by a variable interval. Demand for money rises at the expense of demand for goods. Excess demand for money eventually is satisfied, but its costs mount up in the forms of falling prices, falling output, and falling employment.

In every recession popular attention focuses on a villain. The latest villain is the "cost-price push," the rise in price that imperfectly competitive sellers force upon their markets not in response to current demand but in anticipation of demand. The cost-price push is characteristic of endemic inflation, but its first consequence is deflationary. It generates excess demand for money so that there is pressure brought to bear upon a monetary authority to underwrite advancing prices with increasing supplies of nominal money. If the monetary authority accedes to pressure, the cost-price push intensifies. If the monetary authority defies pressure, excess demand for money at inflated prices punishes output and employment.

Awkward manipulation of nominal money is the final source of monetary instability. Any monetary authority makes its decisions on the basis of information that is incomplete and not altogether accurate or timely. The authority in our monetary system is handicapped by technically imperfect controls. The authority cannot see clearly the road that the monetary system should travel and, in comparison with ideal designs, the steering devices are primitive. We do not have fingertip control of money, with the result that the best-laid plans for management of M can miscarry, and widen the supply-demand gap of monetary disequilibrium.

In the light of monetary experience, it appears that many of us have romanticized monetary control. It is an illusion that the money supply can be manipulated, according to the daily flux of economic statistics and their translation by men of refined intuition, into continuous equilibrium. The limit of feasibility is to ascertain the trend rate of growth in demand for money at a given price level and to set the money supply automatically on the same course. Some may ask: In a serious economic recession, should not the monetary authorities be required to augment the money supply even *more* than this rule would call for? The answer is "no." When the *nominal* supply of money is growing at a stable rate, a serious recession would itself generate a very large increase in *real* money. If the door is opened even slightly to discretionary monetary management, there is no point at which it can be closed.

The Demand Standard in Action · By the rule of the Demand Standard, the nominal supply of money would be increased at a constant rate compounded annually. The rate would be adjusted only with Congressional assent, since full and free debate on the matter of long-run price inflation or deflation is no less important than full and free debate on such issues as tax burdens or labor policy or foreign aid.

The technical procedures of adding to the stock of money should be no more difficult to establish than the procedures of extracting tax payments from the community for subsequent spending under the government budget. Monetary expansion could be a daily, weekly, or monthly "spending" by the monetary system. It could be adapted to seasonal instabilities in demand for money balances.

Demand for money would grow parallel with the money supply in the long run, but its growth line would rise and fall in shorter periods. In each recession, the combination of an increasing money supply and a decreasing demand for money would generate excess supply of money. In each cyclic boom, the combination of increasing money supply and still more rapidly increasing demand for money would generate a shortage in money. Both recession and boom would call forth automatically the kind of imbalance between supply of and demand for money that is cyclically corrective. No one has a principle for doing any better by discretionary means.

On various pretexts, each important user of "credit" would be able to make an eloquent case for some expansion of the money supply in his behalf. The Treasury would request support of new issues. Agriculture would expect credit accommodation for crop movements. Business, large or small, would cry out its need for "capital," and consumers would remember when banks courted their demands for loan funds to spend on cars, houses, and appliances. No sympathy should be wasted on any of these complaints, because giving in to it would mean a demonstrably inflationary acceleration in the growth rate of money.

It is no more difficult to administer orderly growth in money than disorderly growth. Every banker is more than a little proud of his ability to turn down credit applications. The automaton of the Demand Standard can be taught to say "no" to any demand upon the monetary system that would violate the basic rule of growth in means of payment.

ANOTHER BUILT-IN STABILIZER

This country takes pride in its built-in stabilizers, the economic balance-wheels that automatically limit our deviations from normal growth. The stabilizers are automatically sensitized to economic instability and go into action against it without forethought, plan, or discretion. It is not a radical proposal that monetary control should be added to the list of self-activating countermeasures against disturbances in the growth process. Two lines of argument favor the proposal. One is that discretionary control of money supply has done badly. The other is that stable growth in money contributes to stable growth in other economic dimensions.

Discretionary Monetary Management Has Had Its Day · On the evidence of our monetary experience since 1914, American money management has not been a success. Over the long period, the money supply M has been inefficiently balanced against money demand $P(kT)$ at relatively stable prices. The long run casts its shadow over shorter periods. In the 1930s the long run had been deflationary, and the mood of deflation restrained short-run recoveries. As we see it now, the long run has been inflationary, and the mood of inflation permeates short-run expectations. There is an hypothesis that chronic inflation is partly to blame for one paradox of the 1957–1958 recession. The paradox is that prices have run uphill against the gravity of deflation. Perhaps the gravity of long-run inflation has exerted the stronger pull.

Our monetary managers have not succeeded in the cyclical short run. Students of business cycles fail to find convincing evidence that business cycles have shortened in duration since 1914. They find considerable evidence that cycles have become more violent, with amplitude of movement increased. I indicated earlier that monetary management has not been delicately attuned to cyclical turning points. It has missed the turns when monetary policy might have been most effective in damping instability.

Our monetary managers have not sensed the need of a growing economy for stability of monetary expectations. The deeds of management have cultivated alternately expectations of inflation and expectations of deflation. As for words, the notion has developed somehow that the monetary authority is privileged to behave as a benevolent despot; that the authority may mask its plans and policies and neglect to advise the community of its plans and intentions; that the community's prospect concerning the balance of supply and demand for money should be confused and uncertain.

If any form of policy should be explicit, out in the open for all to see, it is monetary policy. There should be certainty of price inflation or certainty of price deflation rather than doubt concerning the monetary atmosphere in which economic plans will materialize. Uncertainty is an impediment to growth. It depresses rational investment, defers gains in productivity, and contributes to the scarcities that policy is supposed to remedy.

The Positive Case for Automatic Monetary Control · The case for automatic control does not rest solely on disillusionment with discretionary control. There are six principal ways in which continuous and stable growth in money can increase the probability of growth in real output at a relatively high rate with minimal perturbations.

1. Stable growth in money lays the foundation for a solvent and efficient payments mechanism. In recurrent inflation, bank capital is sharply reduced relative to bank assets and deposits. Each deflation undermines bank capital through deterioration in asset quality. Our own banking system is propped upright, at public expense, by various devices that are presumed to be adequate substitutes for private investment in banking. Each of these devices has originated during violent movements in the money supply.

2. Stable growth in money supplied and demanded removes one hazard of private or governmental economic planning. That is uncertainty about the length of the monetary yardstick that planners use to measure prospective costs and revenues. Our own monetary system provides us with a yardstick, the value of the dollar, that has been shrinking for sixty years. Steady shrinkage at a constant rate is tolerable and certainly not as damaging to the planning process as shrinkage by fits and starts. Our yardstick has been rubberized, stretching out in each deflation and snapping back in each bout we have with inflation.

3. Stable growth in money avoids the inflations that distort the form of real capital accumulation, and it relieves the economic system of the interruptions in capital formation that result when deflation is applied as the remedy for inflation. Deflation does not undo damage done by inflation: it compounds the damage. During inflation savings are used wastefully on capital projects that are made to seem worthwhile by advancing prices. During deflation savings are destroyed by underemployment of men and resources. Savings misapplied or lost are never recoverable.

4. Stable growth in money and stability in the price level create a favorable environment for flexible individual prices and price relationships. General price deflation results in specific price rigidities, usually in the form of price floors. It invites combination in restraint of price adjustments downward. General price inflation produces its own crop of controlled or admin-

istered prices. The controls may be ceilings imposed by buyers or escalators dictated by sellers. Flexibility of the price level promotes rigidity of price relationships. Since a private-enterprise society relies upon flexible price relationships to allocate resources and guide demands, flexible price levels reduce its growth potential.

5. Stable growth of money and stability in the price level diminish social conflict. Deflation in the last century was politically and socially divisive. Inflation in this century has helped to cleave the population into pressure groups. Any pronounced swing in the price level incites an organized March on Washington and concessions to noisy claimants for special advantage. When price levels are on the move, rational competition of the market place loses out to passionate competition for political leverage.

6. Steady growth in money contributes to development of orderly financial arrangements throughout the community. Deflation creates its distinctive pattern of debt, financial assets, and financial institutions. Inflation gives rise to a different pattern. Debtors are affected by a consideration that should not occur to them—the chance of windfall gain by inflation, of windfall loss by deflation. Creditors pick and choose their financial assets not solely according to debtors' real productivity but also according to debtors' vulnerability to unstable price levels. Loanable funds are allocated inefficiently among borrowers through a financial mechanism that is unduly intricate and expensive.

Stable growth in money minimizes financial distractions in the growth process. Stop-and-go growth in money, dignified as "monetary management," is a nervous tic in the economic system that diverts to finance attention and resources that should be spent on real aspects of development. Money is at its best when it is unobtrusive, its supply increasing according to a firm rule that is known to everyone.

The Folly of Monetary Rules

PAUL A. SAMUELSON

In his 1962 testimony to the Canadian Royal Commission on Banking and Finance, Professor Samuelson offered these criticisms of rules like those espoused by Shaw in the preceding selection.

I MUST FIRMLY disassociate myself from the small but important group of writers who, agreeing that money will not run itself, go on to argue that it ought to be determined permanently by certain automatic formulas. Sometimes this is put in the fancy language of "rules versus authorities," or "laws versus men," or "automaticity versus discretionary action." Of course no one, myself included, will admit to favoring abritrary caprice of bungling rulers over the even-handed justice of well-formulated rules. If every form of explicit cooperative action set up by the men is bound to be completely nearsighted, venal, and blundering, then recourse to astrological rules might pragmatically be defended— although no wise man could have any secure belief that such bungling human beings would ever bind themselves and stay bound to such arbitrary mechanisms. The vicissitudes of ancient coin standards—which were at the mercy of the accidental discovery of precious metals in Latin America, Australia, California, Alaska, South Africa, and now Soviet Russia—would certainly be preferable to some forms of "managed money." In practice though, there have always been—both for good and evil—substantial departures from any automatic coin, bullion, or other kind of gold standard. In principle the choice has never been between discretionary and nondiscretionary action: for when men set up a definitive mechanism which is to run forever after by itself, that involves a single act of discretion which transcends both in its arrogance and its capacity for potential harm any repeated acts of foolish discretion that can be imagined. The relevant choices have to be made pragmatically in terms of the goodness or badness of behavior patterns that result from various kinds of discretionary action.

THE FOLLY OF A PRE-ORDAINED STIPULATED TREND IN MONEY SUPPLY

Specifically consider the suggestion of a money supply which is to grow at exactly 3 percent per year, a policy advocated by some who think no other actions would then be required. Suppose this had been enacted in the United States in 1958, without knowledge of the balance-of-payments problems just ahead and without knowledge of the massive shift to time deposits such as we have been experiencing both as a result of raised interest-rate ceilings on such deposits and the national shift to such deposits as interest rates generally rise. The results would have been quite bad in comparison with what actually happened; and if the balance-of-payments situation had for unpredictable reasons been a great deal worse, the results could have been disastrous. I realize the adherents of such proposals will argue: such dire results might have been avoided if there had been floating exchange rates, perfectly flexible wage rates, and never, never any interest-rate or other ceilings. But since we do not and shall not live in such a never-never land, legislating part of the package would surely do more harm than good.

MONEY CONTROL AND AGGREGATE SPENDING

There are thousands of reasons why any automatic gadget can be improved upon by decision-makers, even by fallible decision-makers. This statement will be denied by those who are firm believers in the ancient Quantity Theory of Money. If it were true *in a causal sense* that there is an invariant relationship between, on the one hand, total dollar income and spending, and, on the other, the supply of money defined in such a way as to be capable of predetermination by the central bank, then an autogyro which kept total money supply growing smoothly would, by hypothesis, keep total money income growing smoothly. While I know that some modern scholars have tried by historical studies to establish an empirical concomitance between money supply and aggregate income, let me simply state here that I find the implied proof of a simple, controllable causal relationship unconvincing.

Suggested Further Readings

Ahearn, Daniel S., *Federal Reserve Policy Reappraised, 1951–1959* (Columbia, 1963).

Andro, Albert, E. Cary Brown, Robert M. Solow, and John Kareken, "Lags in Fiscal and Monetary Policy," in the Commission on Money and Credit, *Stabilization Policies* (Prentice-Hall, 1963).

Brown, E. Cary, "Fiscal Policy in the Thirties: A Reappraisal," *American Economic Review*, LVI (1956).

Brownlee, Oswald, and Alfred Conrad, "Effects upon the Distribution of Income of a Tight Money Policy," in the Commission on Money and Credit, *Stabilization Policy* (Prentice-Hall, 1963).

Committee for Economic Development, *Reducing Tax Rates for Production and Growth* (December 1962).

———, *Taxes and the Budget* (1947).

Culbertson, J. M., *Full Employment or Stagnation?* (McGraw Hill, 1964).

Friedman, Milton, *Studies in the Quantity Theory of Money* (Chicago, 1960).

——— and David Meiselman, "The Relative Stability of Monetary Velocity and the Investment Multiplier in the United States, 1897–1958," in the Commission on Money and Credit, *Stabilization Policies* (Prentice-Hall, 1963).

Gordon, Robert Aaron, *Business Fluctuations*, 2d ed. (Harper, 1961).

Gurley, John, *Financial Aspects of Postwar Economic Developments in the United States*, Study Paper No. 14, U.S. Congress, Joint Economic Committee (January 1960).

Hansen, Alvin H., *Economic Issues of the 1960's* (McGraw Hill, 1960).

Harris, Seymour E., *Economics of the Kennedy Years* (Harper, 1964).

Hickman, Bert G., *Growth and Stability of the Postwar Economy* (Brookings, 1960).

Holmans, A. E., *United States Fiscal Policy, 1945–1959* (Oxford, 1961).

Levy, Michael E., *Fiscal Policy, Cycles, and Growth* (National Industrial Conference Board, 1963).

Lewis, Wilfred, Jr., *Federal Fiscal Policy in the Postwar Recessions* (Brookings, 1962).

Mayer, Thomas, "The Inflexibility of Monetary Policy," *Review of Economics and Statistics*, vol. 40 (1958).

Okun, Arthur M., "Monetary Policy, Debt Management and Interest Rates: A Quantitative Appraisal," in the Commission on Money and Credit, *Stabilization Policies* (Prentice-Hall, 1963).

President's Committee to Appraise Employment and Unemployment Statistics, *Measuring Employment and Unemployment* (Government Printing Office, 1962).

Rosa, Robert V., "Interest Rates and the Central Bank," in Robert Henry

Williams, *Money, Trade, and Economic Growth* (Macmillan, 1951).

Schultze, Charles L., *Recent Inflation in the United States*, Study Paper No. 1, U.S. Congress, Joint Economic Committee (September 1959).

Smith, Warren L., *Debt Management in the United States*, Study Paper No. 19, U.S. Congress, Joint Economic Committee (January 1960).

Tobin, James, "Liquidity Preference and Monetary Policy," *Review of Economics and Statistics*, vol. 29 (1947).

————, "Monetary Policy and the Management of the Public Debt: The Patman Inquiry," *Review of Economics and Statistics*, vol. 35 (1953).

U.S. Congress, Joint Economic Committee, *Higher Employment Rates, 1957–60: Structural Transformation or Inadequate Demand* (1961). *Staff Report on Employment, Growth, and Price Levels* (1959). *The Relationship of Prices to Economic Growth and Stability* (1958). *Federal Expenditure Policy for Economic Stability* (1955).

White, William H., "The Flexibility of Anticyclical Monetary Policy," *Review of Economics and Statistics*, vol. 43 (May 1961).